A Profile of the Automobile and Motor Vehicle Industry

A Profile of the Automobile and Motor Vehicle Industry

Innovation, Transformation, Globalization

James M. Rubenstein

A Profile of the Automobile and Motor Vehicle Industry: Innovation, Transformation, Globalization

First published in 2014 by
Business Expert Press, LLC
222 East 46th Street, New York, NY 10017
www.businessexpertpress.com

ISBN-13: 978-1-60649-536-0 (paperback)
ISBN-13: 978-1-60649-537-7 (e-book)

Business Expert Press Industry Profiles Collection

Collection ISSN: Forthcoming (print)
Collection ISSN: Forthcoming (electronic)

Cover and interior design by Exeter Premedia Services Private Ltd., Chennai, India

First edition: 2014

10 9 8 7 6 5 4 3 2 1

Printed in the United States of America.

Abstract

The motor vehicle industry is one of the world's largest. More than 1 billion vehicles are in use around the world, and 80 million are produced and sold annually. Motor vehicles—including passenger cars, trucks, and commercial vehicles such as buses and taxis—are the principal means by which people and goods are transported within and between most communities in the world.

The motor vehicle industry includes corporations that design, develop, and manufacture cars and trucks. These carmakers, such as Ford and Toyota, are among the world's most-familiar corporate brands. The motor vehicle industry also encompasses lesser-known businesses, including several thousand parts makers, tens of thousands of retailers, and specialized lending agencies.

The importance of the motor vehicle industry transcends even its central role in the global economy. The industry was responsible for many of the fundamental innovations of 20th century production, such as corporate organization, manufacturing processes, and labor relations, as well as sales innovations, such as product branding and consumer financing. In the 21st century, the motor vehicle industry has been a leader in adopting new production strategies and expanding into new markets.

Keywords

auto industry, motor vehicles, cars, trucks, carmakers, auto alley

Contents

List of Figures

List of Tables

CHAPTER 1

Introduction to the Motor Vehicle Industry

The production of motor vehicles is one of the world's largest industrial sectors. Four of the world's five largest manufacturing corporations are carmakers. Annual sales of motor vehicles amount to roughly $2 billion worldwide. More than 1 billion vehicles are in use around the world, and more than 80 million have been produced and sold annually beginning in 2012.

Motor vehicles are the principal means by which people and goods are transported within and between most communities in the world. Most other business sectors depend on motor vehicles to receive their required inputs, to deliver their products and services, and to be accessible to their customers, clients, and employees. The motor vehicle industry is intimately intertwined with the fate of other major industrial sectors, such as energy and steel, as well as retailing and other service sectors.

The importance of the motor vehicle industry transcends even its central role in the global economy. The industry was responsible for many of the fundamental innovations of 20th-century production—such as corporate organization, manufacturing processes, and labor relations—as well as sales innovations—such as product branding and consumer financing. In the 21st century, the motor vehicle industry has been a leader in adopting new production strategies and expanding into new markets.

This book describes the principal elements in the production and sale of motor vehicles, and explains the factors underlying historical and contemporary production and sales patterns. Information is drawn from around the world, with emphasis on North America, especially historical material.

Although this book focuses on the practical business components of motor vehicle production and sales, it is important to note at the outset that motor vehicles play a more central role in modern society than contributing to the conduct of business. People around the world have what has often been described, for a lack of a better phrase, a love affair with motor vehicles. Motor vehicles play a central role in popular culture as well as personal recreation and entertainment. The specific vehicle that a consumer chooses to purchase displays personal preferences, emotions, and values. Vehicles may differ only in relatively minor details of styling and performance, yet these minor variations reflect the individual's social status and taste.

The United States has more registered motor vehicles than licensed drivers. Given that an individual can drive only one vehicle at a time, if a motor vehicle was no more than a practical conveyance, demand for vehicles would not logically exceed the supply of licensed drivers. Meanwhile, owning a motor vehicle is arguably the single most important aspiration among people living in developing countries—most notably Chinese—as was the case with North Americans and Europeans in previous generations.

The motor vehicle industry includes corporations that design, develop, and manufacture cars and trucks. These carmakers, such as Ford and Toyota, are among the world's most-familiar corporate brands. The motor vehicle industry also encompasses less well-known businesses, including thousands of parts makers, which fabricate the thousands of vehicle parts at thousands of factories. At the other end of the carmakers' production lines are tens of thousands of retailers and specialized lending agencies. Motor vehicle production is also considered to have an extremely high multiplier effect on local service industries. A vehicle factory employing several thousand direct production workers generates demand for services such as food, cleaning, materials, and supplies.

Some Terminology

Vehicles are classified as light, medium, or heavy. This book focuses on light vehicles, which are defined as weighing less than 10,000 pounds. Light vehicles account for 95% of total vehicle sales worldwide. The light vehicle market is divided between passenger cars and light trucks (known outside North America as light commercial vehicles). Medium- and heavy-duty vehicles, which include large trucks and buses, are included in some production data, but the volume is not large enough to significantly affect global patterns and trends.

The North American Industrial Classification System (NAICS) has two four-digit codes that cover a large share of the motor vehicle industry. NAICS 3361 is motor vehicle manufacturing (essentially assembly plants) and NAICS 3363 is motor vehicle parts manufacturing. Within NAICS 3361 and 3363, specific types of assembly and parts operations are broken down into six- and eight-digit code levels. However, a number of key vehicle parts are not included in NAICS 3363, including bodies, paint, glass, and tires. NAICS 3363 also does not provide an accurate picture of motor vehicle production because it includes parts for both new vehicles and for replacement in older vehicles.

Light vehicles are manufactured by corporations that are referred to here as carmakers even though they produce light trucks as well as passenger cars. In North America, three carmakers—Chrysler Group, Ford Motor Company, and General Motors Company (GM)—are known as the "Detroit Three," and other companies are referred to as international or foreign carmakers. Ford and GM, founded in the first decade of the 20th century, were the two best-selling North American carmakers in 1910, and remained so in most years since. Chrysler, organized in the 1920s, quickly joined Ford and GM as sales leaders. With most of the smaller U.S. carmakers forced out of business in the 1930s during the Great Depression, Chrysler, Ford, and GM became known as the Big Three. At their peak in the 1950s, the Big Three sold 95% of the vehicles in North America.

Japanese-owned companies rapidly gained market share in North America during the late 20th century, especially by offering energy-efficient vehicles in the wake of the 1970s petroleum shortages and price rises. During the first decade of the 21st century, as their combined market share dipped below 50%, and Chrysler's sales fell below first Toyota's and then Honda's, the term Big Three became obsolete. The term Detroit Three replaced Big Three because Chrysler, Ford, and GM have headquarters in the Detroit metropolitan area—GM in the Renaissance Center in downtown Detroit, Ford in the suburb of Dearborn, and Chrysler 20 kilometers north of Detroit in Auburn Hills.

A carmaker markets a vehicle under a brand name, which the motor vehicle industry refers to as a "make." All of the major carmakers sell more than one make. Confusingly, each major carmaker, with the exception of GM, offers a make that is identical to the corporate name and others that are not. Hence, one of Toyota Motor Company's makes is Toyota, and one of Ford Motor Company's makes is Ford. However, Toyota Motor Company also sells a make named Lexus, and Ford Motor Company also sells a make named Lincoln. GM does not market a make that shares its corporate name but, like the other carmakers, has several makes that use other names such as Chevrolet and Cadillac.

Carmakers divide their makes into what are known in the United States as models or nameplates. The Ford Motor Company's Ford make, for example, has a Focus model and a Fusion model. The Fusion is much larger than the Focus, and the two are not built in the same factories. In British English, a model is sometimes referred to as a "marque," which is the French term. Rather than "model," the German carmaker BMW prefers the term "series," as in 3 Series, 5 Series, and 7 Series. Daimler-Benz prefers "class," as in the C Class, E Class, and S Class models.

Models may differ from one another substantially, but not always. For example, Ford has models called C-Max and Escape, which look very different from the Focus but are closely related mechanically. Carmakers also market virtually identical models under different names in different parts of the world. For example, the model that Ford markets as Fusion in North America is sold with the Mondeo nameplate in the rest of the world. Carmakers also sell very similar vehicles under different makes. For example, Ford Motor Company's Ford make includes a Fusion model, and its Lincoln make has an MKZ model that differs modestly from the Fusion. Ultimately, a carmaker must choose which makes more sense financially—to market two vehicles as a single model or to incur the heavy costs of advertising them as two distinct models. Two different model names may increase marketing costs, but the carmaker may profit by selling a lot more with two model names rather than one because it can attract very different cohorts of customers to the two distinct models.

Vehicles are also organized by platform, which is the architectural underpinnings of the vehicle, primarily the frame, axles, and other chassis parts. For example, the Ford Fusion shares a platform with the Mondeo, Edge, S-Max, and Galaxy. The Edge, a low-slung sport utility vehicle reminiscent of a station wagon, is sold in North America. The S-Max and Galaxy, tall multipurpose vehicles reminiscent of a North American minivan, are sold in Europe. In order to recoup the billions of dollars in research and development expenses, carmakers try to design a single platform that can be utilized to manufacture numerous models that are clearly differentiated and aimed at very different groups of consumers.

Within each model, carmakers distinguish trim levels. A trim level is a distinctive package of comfort and performance features. Ford's Fusion model, for example, includes an S trim level and an SE trim level. Features that appear on the SE trim but not the S trim include power seat adjusters, keyless entry, satellite radio, and heated exterior mirrors.

In 1913, one-half of the vehicles in the world were a single make and a single model, the Ford Model T. In 2013, the French magazine *Auto Moto* identified 86 makes and 3,000 models available around the world. The models ranged from a 3-meter long Tata Nano with a 2-cylinder 0.6 liter engine costing $3,000, to a 6-meter long Rolls Royce Phantom with a 12-cylinder 6.8 liter engine costing $400,000. With so many models, the average production volume per model of less than 30,000 per year was far below the level needed to profitably operate a factory or amortize the high costs of development of a new model. However, carmakers figure that if a variety of models can be designed so that they can be manufactured on a single platform, the combined output will be profitable.

Organization of the Book

Chapter 2 discusses the operations and history of the motor vehicle industry. Carmakers undertake three principal operations: assembly of vehicles, research and development of new and revised models, and marketing. Other actors actually sell the vehicles and produce most of the parts.

The first practical motor vehicles were built in Europe during the late 19th century. Key vehicle components, such as the internal combustion engine and the rubber tire, were also developed in Europe. U.S. companies dominated global production and sales of motor vehicles beginning in the early 20th century. Key pioneers included Ransom E. Olds, Henry Ford, and William C. Durant. Large-volume production of motor vehicles diffused to other economically developed regions, notably Europe and Japan, during the middle of the 20th century and to developing regions, especially Asia and Latin America, during the late 20th century and into the 21st century.

Chapters 3 and 4 summarize the organization of the motor vehicle industry, with production of vehicles discussed in Chapter 3 and vehicle sales in Chapter 4. The production of vehicles is concentrated in the hands of a few carmakers. Ten carmakers are responsible for three-fourths of the world's motor vehicle production. Two are based in the United States (Ford and General Motors), four in Asia (Toyota, Hyundai, Honda, and Suzuki), and four in Europe (Volkswagen, Renault, PSA Peugeot Citroën, and Fiat). Because Renault has a controlling interest in Asia-based Nissan, data for Nissan are included with Renault in this book. Similarly, data for U.S.-based Chrysler are included here with Fiat, which controls it. These companies all produce and sell vehicles in more than one region of the world. Very high capital costs are a strong barrier to entry for new large-scale producers.

Globally, nearly 95% of motor vehicles are produced in three regions: Asia, Europe, and North America. Asia, including China, Japan, India, and South Korea, is responsible for 44% of the world total, and China is by far the world's largest vehicle producer. Within these three regions, most vehicle production is highly clustered. Within North America, most production is clustered in a north–south corridor known as auto alley that extends from southwestern Ontario and Michigan to northern Alabama and Mississippi. Within Europe, most production is on an east-west axis between England and Russia and centered on Germany.

Unionization has been an important element in the development of the motor vehicle industries in Europe and North America. Over many decades, unionized auto workers have negotiated contracts with relatively high wages and benefits. Asia-based carmakers have no distinctive work rules, which has facilitated more flexible production methods. In recent years, competitors based in North America and Europe have introduced Asia-inspired flexible work rules into union environments.

Chapter 4 focuses on the sales of motor vehicles. Most vehicles are assembled in the same region in which they are sold. International trade of vehicles consists primarily of shipments from East Asia, especially Japan and South Korea, to other regions. Underlying the geographic footprint are economies of scale, which are obtained at roughly 200,000 annual capacity for assembly plants.

For most consumers, a motor vehicle is the most expensive product they purchase, with the exception of a house. Carmakers do not sell directly to consumers. Instead, vehicles are sold through independently owned dealers, who have purchased franchises to sell a carmaker's vehicles in a specific market area. Independently owned dealers also sell used vehicles. Most consumers borrow money to purchase new vehicles, and carmakers have established credit companies to facilitate consumer loans.

The light vehicle market is divided between passenger cars and light trucks. More than 80% of light vehicle sales are passenger cars worldwide, but in North America light trucks account for nearly half of sales. Passenger cars are further divided into market segments commonly designated by letters of the alphabet. The smallest vehicles are designated "A." The most popular segments are "C" and "D" in North America and "B" and "C" in the rest of the world. Carmakers typically sell particular models for several years; research and development for new models are expensive, multiyear undertakings.

Chapter 5 examines outside forces affecting the production of motor vehicles. Of most consequence for carmakers is the fact that the suppliers of parts are responsible for more than 70% of the value added of a motor vehicle. Parts suppliers are organized in tiers. Supplying a carmaker typically are several hundred tier one parts manufacturers, most of which make large complex modules such as seats and instrument panels. Tier two parts makers supply tier one parts makers, and tier three parts makers in turn supply tier two parts makers. Most parts are produced in the same regional clusters as the final assembly plants. Some parts, especially those made by lower tier suppliers, are produced in low-wage countries and shipped to plants operated by tier one parts makers near the final assembly plants.

Carmakers are also major purchasers of raw materials and commodities, discussed in detail in other books in this series. Steel is the principal raw material in motor vehicles, roughly one-half by weight, although the proportion is decreasing. Plastic, aluminum, rubber, fluids, and glass are other important raw materials. The motor vehicle industry is also a major user of high-value trace elements such as platinum and zinc. Motor vehicle producers and parts makers contract with steelmakers and suppliers of other raw materials. Negotiations are inevitably challenging, with carmakers seeking to minimize price and source globally whereas raw materials suppliers seek higher prices.

Historically, motor vehicle industry was one of the world's most vertically integrated industrial sectors. Ford and GM, in particular, were known for controlling all elements of the production process from raw materials through finished vehicles. The level of vertical integration has declined sharply, yet it is still relatively high compared to most industrial sectors. Parts makers have taken on more responsibility in the production process. Parts makers produce large modules and deliver them to the final assembly plant on a just-in-time basis, only moments before needed. Carmakers traditionally awarded contracts to the lowest bidder on an annual basis. Now, carmakers offer parts makers multiyear contracts and select them on the basis of highest quality rather than lowest price.

Chapter 6 reviews the regulatory framework within which the motor vehicle industry operates. Government mandates address primarily three areas of concern: safety, emissions, and fuel efficiency. The earliest government regulations, such as licensing drivers and traffic controls, were aimed at making driving safer. Beginning in the 1960s, carmakers were required to equip vehicles with such safety features as seatbelts and impact-absorbing bumpers. During the same period, vehicles were required to have devices to control noxious emissions. In response to Middle East oil shocks beginning in the 1970s, vehicles have been required to meet minimum fuel efficiency standards.

Carmakers have been subject to government management and even direct ownership in some cases. Governments own significant stakes of carmakers in China. Several of the major carmakers based in Europe were majority government owned in the past, and government stakes continue in some. Developing countries have viewed investment in the auto industry to be a major component of economic development strategies. In North America, GM and Chrysler went into and out of government-managed bankruptcy protection in 2009.

Chapter 7 discusses challenges and opportunities facing the motor vehicle industry. On the supply side, the principal challenge is to produce alternative-fuel vehicles. Several alternative sources of power to the gasoline-powered internal combustion engine are being actively pursued.

Vehicles powered by electricity have become widely available for the first time in more than a century. Hybrid gas-electric vehicles may capture a large share of the market in the years ahead. Other possible power sources include biofuel, hydrogen, and natural gas. Carmakers are challenged to find the mix of fuel types that best meets market demand and fuel efficiency standards. The amount and distribution of reserves of scarce metals and other resources, in addition to petroleum, continue to challenge carmakers.

On the supply side, vehicle sales are increasing rapidly in developing countries, especially in Asia. Carmakers are challenged to enter or expand production in emerging markets. At the same time, demand is stagnant in developed countries. Whether this stagnation reflects a cyclical pattern—that is, a function of the lingering effects of a severe recession—or structural change—reduced interest by younger people in owning vehicles—is debated by industry analysts.

Electronics play an increasing role in the performance of vehicle engines and in providing increased safety. Carmakers and regulators are struggling to offer appropriate electronic convenience features, such as access to social media, Internet, and e-mail. In the long run, driverless vehicles may become common. Technological capabilities are already in place. Consumer behavior and regulatory issues are the principal constraints to the diffusion of self-driving vehicles.

CHAPTER 2

Operation of the Motor Vehicle Industry

The motor vehicle industry encompasses a large number of actors. At the center of the industry are a small number of corporations, most of which include the word "Motor" as part of their name. Informally, these corporations are usually called automakers or carmakers even though they typically manufacture trucks as well as cars. Ten carmakers are responsible for producing and selling nearly three-fourths of the world's motor vehicles. The names of these carmakers rank among the world's products with the highest consumer recognition. This chapter and the next two focus on these few carmakers.

The handful of carmakers are supported by thousands of manufacturers of parts and commodities that go into the fabrication of vehicles. A car contains between 10,000 and 30,000 parts, depending on the vehicle and the counting method.[1] (Does each screw count as a separate part? Is a piston one part or six?) Roughly 70% of the value added in the manufacture of a motor vehicle is accounted for by the several thousand independent suppliers, leaving only 30% for the carmakers. At the other end of the production process, the actual sale of vehicles is handled by many tens of thousands of independent dealers. The parts supply sector of the industry is discussed in Chapter 5 and the distribution sector in Chapter 4.

Principal Activities of Carmakers

A carmaker undertakes three principal types of operations. First, it operates assembly plants, which are large factories where thousands of parts are put together into finished vehicles. Second, it conducts extensive research and development operations prior to the decision to manufacture a particular vehicle. Third, it coordinates marketing operations to make the public aware of the attributes of its particular models.

Assembly Operations

A typical assembly plant is built with the capacity to turn out approximately one finished vehicle per minute, sixty vehicles per hour. With two eight-hour daily shifts of workers, that speed works out to an annual output of roughly one-quarter million vehicles. Some assembly plants can achieve a higher output by scheduling a third shift, although a continuous three-shift operation makes it difficult to schedule down time for maintenance and repairs. Some assembly plants double output by adding a second line, that is, essentially running two assembly operations under one roof.

Worldwide, approximately 275 assembly plants produce at least 100,000 vehicles annually on a regular basis. Several hundred other assembly plants either produce a smaller number of vehicles by design, or operate regularly at less than half of capacity. Most assembly plants are located in regions of the world that minimize the cost of shipping to customers (Figure 2.1). The adage in the motor vehicle industry is "build them where you sell them."

Motor vehicle assembly is a classic example of an industry that locates in accordance with Alfred Weber's industrial location theory. In his *Theory of the Location of Industries*, published in German in 1909, Weber argued that the optimal location for a factory is the point that minimizes the aggregate costs of bringing in raw materials and shipping out finished products. If the cost of bringing in raw materials is less than the cost of shipping out finished products, according to Weber, then the optimal location for a factory is pulled relatively close to the customers. Car assembly is such an example: a large number of relatively compact parts are fabricated into a final product that is relatively bulky, fragile, and expensive to ship to customers, so assembly operations are optimally located close to customers.

The fundamental operation of the assembly plant has not changed dramatically since the Ford Motor Company's innovations in the early 20th century. Before Ford's innovations, a vehicle was assembled in a

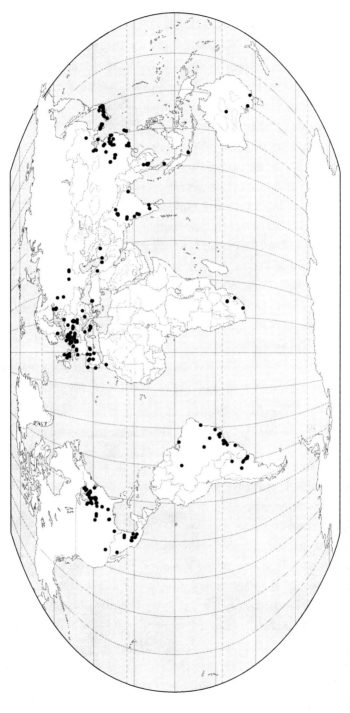

Figure 2.1 Motor vehicle assembly plants with annual production above 100,000 vehicles

single spot in the factory, with most operations performed as the partially assembled vehicle sat on sawhorses. Each type of tool and machine was stored in a particular location elsewhere in the factory. Materials to perform a particular machining operation would be carried through the factory to the machine. When a particular tool was needed, it was retrieved from its specified location, carried to the partially assembled vehicle, and returned to storage when no longer needed.

Ford's first innovation was to arrange in a logical sequence each operation needed to assemble a vehicle, as well as the tools and machinery needed to complete each operation. In an era when factories occupied multiple stories, Ford opened a four-story assembly plant in 1910 in Highland Park, Michigan, in which relatively light-weight parts, such as upholstery and wheels, were made on the upper two floors, and the heavier parts, such as bodies and engines, on the lower two floors. The specific types of tools and machinery needed to complete a particular operation were placed where the operation was performed in the Highland Park assembly plant, rather than grouped together in one storage area, as was the case in older assembly plants.

Ford's second innovation was the moving assembly line, installed at Highland Park over a one-year period of trial-and-error experiments in 1913 and 1914, beginning with specific operations, and ultimately extending to the entire production process. A continuously moving belt carried partially completed vehicles from one station to the next, permitting each task to be performed by groups of workers positioned along in a logical sequence. Needed parts, materials, tools, and machines for each operation were either placed within reach of the workers, or brought to them on the moving line.

Modern assembly plants have refined the logical sequencing of the operations and the design of the individual tasks performed along the moving line, but the fundamental structure of the production process introduced by Ford a century ago is still used in nearly all assembly plants. The principal exception is a handful of assembly plants that produce small volumes of luxury or sports cars.

An assembly plant is typically divided into three main sets of operations. The first is the body build-up. The sides, roof, and fenders are welded to the frame to create the body. Most of the welding of the frame is done by robots. Doors, hood, and trunk panels are stamped from steel or molded from plastic and hung onto the body. The body panels are sometimes stamped at separate facilities and shipped to the assembly plants although in some cases, the stamping facility is adjacent to the assembly plant. The end result of this first set of operations is known as a "body-in-white." Most vehicles are built through unitized construction, which involves welding the frame of front, rear, and side rails into an underbody. Top and side frames are then welded to the underbody to form a shell.

The second set of operations occurs in the paint shop. The body is cleaned, primed with an undercoat, painted in one of many colors, baked, and sealed with a protective coating. The coating operations, like the body build-up, are done primarily by robots. To assure a clean, even coat, the vehicles pass through sealed chambers that are inaccessible to visitors and even to most employees. Typically, a primer layer is applied to steel and plastic components to smooth out irregularities and imperfections and to improve resistance to chipping. A basecoat layer provides most of the coloring. A final clearcoat layer provides most of the protection. The coatings are often applied through electrocoating, in which the body parts are electrically charged and immersed in a bath consisting of oppositely charged deionized water. The paint particles are attracted to the surface, neutralized, and baked into a film.

The third set of operations in an assembly plant is the final assembly. The painted body moves along a constantly moving assembly line at a rate of roughly one per minute. As the body passes each work station, one or more workers attach a particular part. The line changes elevation depending on the part to be installed. The engine and transmission are inserted from below. The doors are removed to facilitate installation of seats, instrument panel, and other interior parts. Glass, wheels, tires, suspension—the various parts are attached in a logical sequence as the vehicle moves along the line. The final step is to turn the ignition and drive away the vehicle. The body drop was the most dramatic and widely photographed feature of Ford's original moving assembly line. Some pickup trucks still have body drop, but most light vehicles are built through unitized construction.

Research and Development Operations

Carmakers update their vehicles every year, sometimes substantially and sometimes merely cosmetically. They introduce entirely new models every few years. The development of a new or substantially revised model takes several years of work at a cost of several billion dollars. Extensive research and development operations precede the introduction of new and improved models.

R&D operations are especially complex in part because many actors with widely varying expertise are involved. The principal actors in vehicle development include:

- product planners, who assess the need for a new or substantially revised vehicle of a particular style at a particular price point;
- market analysts, who identify the demographic characteristics of the primary targeted customers such as age group, gender, income, and place of residence;
- stylists, who design the exterior and interior appearance of the vehicle;
- advanced engineers, who develop broad parameters such as engine size, dimensions, and weight;
- detail engineers, who develop specifications for particular parts of the vehicle such as the engine, transmission, and body;
- consumer surveyors, who analyze customer reaction to proposed designs and features of the vehicle;
- financial analysts, who calculate the potential return on investment of the new vehicle and the impact of varying design and engineering concepts on the vehicle's profitability;
- production engineers, who design tool, dies, and machinery needed to assemble the vehicle;
- factory managers, who determine the arrangements of the facilities that will ultimately assemble the vehicle; and
- quality control experts, who test the vehicle and the individual parts to assure their performance even under extreme conditions.

The various actors must frequently adjudicate among differing perspectives because the training and priorities of one set of actors may not result in the same preferences as those of other actors. For example, engineers may push for use of a part that financial analysts calculate is not cost effective, consumer analysts demonstrate is unimportant to customers, and production engineers determine is too complicated to actually manufacture. An innovative style may be shot down by unfavorable reactions from the consumer researchers, engineers, and financial analysts. Team members may be pulled between the judgment of other team members and the judgment of the supervisors in their functional areas of expertise.

R&D operations are also complex because the marketing, engineering, management, and finance people working on one project must communicate with their counterparts working on other current or recently completed projects. Because of the high cost of developing new and revised vehicles, the project teams seek to share as many parts as possible to save money. Factory-level production and management team members work to ensure that the new vehicle is as compatible as possible with existing vehicles already being built in the company's assembly plants. Marketing-oriented team members seek a clear and distinct market niche in order to minimize overlap and cannibalizing of other projects.

Yet, even as vehicles have become more complex, and the development process has involved more diverse contributors, carmakers have substantially reduced the amount of time needed to develop vehicles. An entirely new vehicle can roll off the assembly line within two or three years of start of development, about half of the time typically needed during the second half of the 20th century. Computer-assisted design and testing as well as allocating more responsibility to the project team, have contributed to the reduction in development time.

Marketing Operations

The third major responsibility of carmakers is to market their vehicles to the public. Carmakers do not sell their products directly to the public, relying instead on independent dealers, as discussed in Chapter 4. Nonetheless, carmakers are among the biggest spenders on advertising. Together, carmakers spent around $14 billion on advertising in the United States in 2012 according to *Advertising Age*. General Motors Company (GM) spent more on advertising in the United States than any other company except Procter & Gamble. Ford ranked seventh, Chrysler fifteenth, and Toyota sixteenth. The automotive industry's spending on advertising included $6 billion for TV; $2 billion for newspapers, magazines, radio, and Internet ads; and $6 billion for search-engine marketing, online videos, and social media.

As a result of heavy spending on advertising for more than a century, carmakers have made their names and those of their individual makes and models among the most recognized of all consumer products. The high cost of creating high name recognition has discouraged carmakers from adopting new names. It has also discouraged them from terminating slow-selling brands.

Through the decades, carmakers have been able to market their vehicles in tune with the changing values and priorities of its customers, and they have embraced the many changes in marketing strategies and advertising media through the 20th century. During the first decade of the 20th century, when the sale of sheet music was a leading method of generating revenue, a popular song *In My Merry Oldsmobile* had a chorus beginning "Come away with me, Lucille / In my merry Oldsmobile." The song both reflected and helped maintain Oldsmobile's position as the first high-volume, low-priced car in the United States. As a GM make between 1908 and 2004, Oldsmobile frequently used the melody in its advertising.

Ford captured half the new-vehicle market in the United States and the world during the 1910s by selling a single model, the Model T. For most of the eighteen-year run of Model T, it was famously produced in only one color, black. The company's newspaper and magazine advertising communicated Henry Ford's vision of the car as a low-cost, practical machine, useful for farm chores and deliveries.

GM passed Ford as the best-selling carmaker during the 1920s by offering vehicles with attractive styling. GM's long-time head Alfred P. Sloan set out to sell what he called "a car for every purse and purpose." GM's marketing strategy worked because it both reflected and shaped the American class structure. GM created a hierarchy of makes, differentiated by price, appealing to people in each social class. A person owning one GM make was instantly identified as belonging to a different social class than an owner of another make. As families became richer and more highly placed in society, they moved up a "ladder of consumption" by trading in their lower status car for a higher status one. In 1955, for example, GM's luxury Cadillac make accounted for 5% of the company's

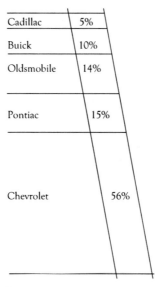

Cadillac	5%
Buick	10%
Oldsmobile	14%
Pontiac	15%
Chevrolet	56%

Figure 2.2 GM's ladder of consumption, 1955. Figures are the percentages of GM's overall sales in 1955 contributed by each make. The makes are displayed with the highest-priced make (Cadillac) at the top rung of the ladder and the lowest-priced make (Chevrolet) at the bottom rung

sales, its lowest-price Chevrolet make accounted for 56%, and its three medium-priced makes between 10% and 15% each (Figure 2.2). GM positioned its products to conform closely to the distribution of U.S. income, with a broad base and narrow top.

GM secured its dominant position in the North American market during the 1950s by advertising heavily on the newly ascendant advertising medium of TV. Popular singers sang "See the USA in your Chevrolet," reinforcing the French pronunciation of the car's last syllable. GM's Pontiac make was advertised to have high performance, Oldsmobile to have advanced technology, Buick to have professional reliability, and Cadillac to have wealthy and powerful owners—this despite the fact that the five makes differed more in appearance than in mechanics.

Carmakers have fashioned their advertising to changing social conventions. During the Roaring 20s, vehicles were marketed to women who had been discouraged from driving until then. Vehicles were advertised to be like jet airplanes in the 1950s, to be part of the counterculture in the 1960s, to be energy efficient in the 1970s, to be built with high quality in the 1980s, and to be rugged in the 1990s. In the early 21st century, carmakers reached out to advertise in media of special interest to African Americans, Hispanics, and gays. Carmakers are now among the leaders in advertising through social media, which is expected to take more than one-half of the automotive industry's advertising budget in the mid-2010s.

History of Motor Vehicle Operations

Nineteenth-century enthusiasts struggled with what to name the new machine. The titles of leading 19th century magazines, such as *Motor Age* and *The Horseless Age*, reflected the uncertainty.

- "Automobile" was constructed in the United States from the French for self and moving. French, in turn, got the word from the Greek *autos* and the Latin *mobilis*. But the French themselves did not adopt the word "automobile," preferring *voiture*, a more general word for vehicle, and the French use the word "auto" as a shortening of *autobus*, the formal term for "bus."
- "Car" comes to the English language through the Celtic *karros* and ultimately from the Latin *carrum*, meaning wheeled vehicle. The British called the new machine a "motor car," now shortened to "car," but for much of the 20th century shortened to "motor." The American use of "car" comes from shortening "horseless carriage." "Carriage" in turn came to English through the French *cariage*, meaning carry.
- "Truck" may have been derived from the Greek word *trochos*, which means wheel. Before the invention of motor vehicles, "truck" referred to a wheeled vehicle suitable for carrying a heavy load. The British most often refer to this type of vehicle as a "lorry." The etymology of "lorry" is unknown, possibly related to a version of *lurry*, a once obscure and now archaic word in a British dialect meaning to pull or drag.
- "Vehicle" comes from the Latin *vehiculum*, another word for carriage or conveyance.

European Pioneers

The United States would become the dominant producer of motor vehicles in the early 20th century, but Europeans were responsible for designing and building the first practical motor vehicles in the 19th century. The Benz Patent Motorwagen has the strongest legal claim to be the world's first gasoline-powered vehicle because Karl Benz (1844–1929) was issued a patent for it in 1886. The Motorwagen was a three-wheeled vehicle made of steel tubing, powered by a four-stroke gasoline engine mounted under the seat and connected by bicycle-style chains to drive the rear wheels.

Gottlieb Daimler (1834–1900) and Wilhelm Maybach (1846–1929) are especially important in the development of the modern internal combustion engine. Daimler was a director and Maybach the chief designer at Deutz-AG-Gasmotorenfabrik, an engine manufacturer half-owned by Nikolaus Otto (1832–1891). In 1877, Otto had patented a four-stroke engine that proved to be the approach used in the gasoline-powered motor vehicle engine. In a four-stroke engine, a piston moves in and out of a cylinder in four stages or strokes:

- The first stroke, intake, fills the cylinder with gasoline, pushing the piston out.
- The second stroke, compression, closes the cylinder, and pushes the piston in, compressing the fuel.
- The third stroke, ignition, ignites the gas in the cylinder, causing the piston to push out.
- The fourth stroke, exhaust, opens the cylinder, draining the spent fuel and letting the piston push in.

Otto's engine proved unreliable and inefficient, so Daimler and Maybach set out to improve it. After disagreements with Otto, they left Deutz and formed their own company. They built a working gasoline-powered engine in 1885 and installed it under a four-wheel carriage a year later, two months after Benz had applied for his patent, but before it had been issued. Working 100 kilometers from each other, Benz and Daimler were unaware of each other's work. The two German neighbors produced rival luxury cars until they merged in 1926.

More than a century before Benz and Daimler's innovations, Nicholas-Joseph Cugnot (1725–1804) built the first self-propelled vehicle large enough and strong enough to carry people. Cugnot's *fardier à vapeur* (steam-powered cart) first ran in 1769. An improved model built two years later, and still operable today, is displayed at the Musée des Arts et Métiers in Paris. Into the 19th century, steam proved more amenable to powering train locomotives and ships than road-driven vehicles. Rail ties and water surfaces offered less friction than the primitive roads of that era, and the considerable amount of time needed to heat up the boiler made steam more suitable for long-distance rail and sea travel than for short road trips.

An 1884 steam-powered de Dion-Bouton et Trépardoux is considered to be the oldest vehicle still driven on public roads (in England). Founded in 1883 by Jules-Albert de Dion (1856–1946), Georges Bouton (1847–1938), and Charles Trépardoux (1853–1920), the French company was a leading steam carmaker in 1900, producing 400 vehicles in that year. A de Dion finished first in the world's first officially organized car race—a 50-kilometer route from Paris to Rouen, France, in 1894—but the judges did not award it the top prize on the grounds that it needed a passenger to stoke the boiler.

Inventors of electric cars include Gustave Trouvé (1839–1902), who demonstrated a three-wheeled vehicle in Paris in 1881, and Andreas Flocken (1845–1913), who built the first four-wheeled vehicle called the Elektrowagen in 1888 in Cobourg, Germany. As the internal combustion engine became the dominant power source in the first decade of the 20th century, the pioneering electric carmakers faded into obscurity.

France was the world leader in motor vehicle production in 1900. That year, 62,000 vehicles were produced worldwide, 30,000 of them in France. The French carmaker Panhard et Levassor was the leading carmaker in 1900, selling 1,000 vehicles that year. Panhard et Levassor, established in 1887 by René Panhard (1841–1908) and Émile Levassor (1843–1897), was responsible for so many key innovations that the standard design of the car became known in the early 20th century as the *Systeme Panhard*. Among the features attributed to Panhard are fitting an engine with four cylinders, mounting the gasoline engine in the front of the vehicle instead of underneath the seat, steering the vehicle with a wheel instead of a tiller, attaching a transmission with gears to the rear wheels, and engaging a clutch to change gears. Panhard et Levassor's car-making operations were acquired by Citroën in 1965.

Leadership Passes to the United States

During the first decade of the 20th century, leadership of the world's auto industry passed from Europe to the United States. Several Americans competed for the recognition of having built the first car in the United States. Among the stronger claims are:

- Gottfried Schloemer (1842–1921) built what may have been the first gasoline-powered car driven in the United States in 1889 in Milwaukee. The engine was ordered by Schloemer from the Sintz Gas Engine Company of Grand Rapids, Michigan.
- Henry Nadig (1843–1930) was widely witnessed driving a horseless carriage in 1889 in Allentown, Pennsylvania. Because his vehicle was disturbing horses, he was ordered to operate it only at night. A replica is displayed in America on Wheels, a transportation museum in Allentown.
- John William Lambert (1860–1952) may have built the first horseless carriage for sale in Ohio City, Ohio, in 1891, but he abandoned the initiative when no customers came forward.
- Charles H. Black (1852–1918) mounted a Benz engine on a carriage and drove it in Indianapolis in 1891. He may have been the first person in the country to be issued a driver's license in Chicago and the first to have paid a claim after causing an accident, both in 1892.
- Elwood P. Haynes (1857–1925) is cited by the *Encyclopaedia Britannica* and the Smithsonian Institution as the second to build and successfully road test a gasoline-powered vehicle in the United States—in Kokomo, Indiana, in 1894—but the first to build a vehicle powered solely by gas rather than capable of also being hitched to a horse.

Overlooking all of the above claims, the Smithsonian and *Britannica* instead give credit for the first successfully road-tested gasoline-powered vehicle in the United States to the vehicle built in 1893 by the brothers Charles E. Duryea (1861–1938) and J. Frank Duryea (1869–1967) in Springfield, Massachusetts. Although probably not actually the first, the Duryea brothers are clearly the preeminent pioneers of the U.S. auto industry for two reasons: (1) they were the first to win an official race in the United States, (2) they were the first to build cars for sale in the United States—and actually sell them.

The first race in the United States was sponsored by the *Chicago Times-Herald* on November 28, 1895. The 52.4 mile (84.3 kilometer) race through the streets of Chicago and Evanston was won by J. Frank Duryea in 10 hours 23 minutes, of which 7 hours 53 minutes were running time. Second place was won by a Benz driven by Oscar B. Mueller. The race was originally set for November 2 from Chicago to Milwaukee, but it was scrubbed because few of the 83 cars entered were actually in the city and operable. Only six cars showed up for the rescheduled race on Thanksgiving Day, and only two finished in the snowy, cold, and muddy conditions.

Taking advantage of the publicity from winning the race, the Duryea Motor Wagon Company became the first company organized for the purpose of building vehicles and selling them to the public. Four were delivered in 1895 and nine more in 1896. The Duryea brothers disagreed over sharing credit between the two of them. Frank was the driver and the sole brother in Springfield as the company was getting started. Charles claimed that the vehicle was based on a model that he had developed several years earlier.

The editors of *Automobile Quarterly* magazine have unearthed more than 3,000 firms organized to build motor vehicles in the United States during the late 1890s and the first years of the 20th century. It is difficult to identify a precise total number of carmakers because few of them ever advanced from building experimental prototypes to producing vehicles for sale.

The two best-selling vehicles in the United States around 1900 were Columbia and Locomobile. The Columbia car was produced by the Pope Manufacturing Company beginning in 1897. Albert A. Pope (1843–1909) established the company in 1877 to manufacture bicycles, and by the dawn of the automotive age, he was known as the King of Bicycles. Records compiled by *Automotive News* attributed to Columbia 100 of a total of 157 cars sold in the United States in 1898 and 440 of 1,049 sold in 1899. Pope spun off Columbia in 1899 as an independent company, but it was snapped up by a holding company called the Electric Vehicle Company (EVC), which was trying to create a monopoly as described in the next section. Pope went on to acquire a number of small carmakers, but none could match the rapid growth of competitors during the first decade of the 20th century. Pope declared bankruptcy during the Panic of 1907, and he exited the auto industry altogether in 1915.

The Locomobile Company of America was founded in 1899 by John B. Walker (1847–1931), editor and publisher of *Cosmopolitan* magazine. According to *Automotive News*, Locomobile accounted for 750 of 2,288 cars sold in the United States in 1900, 1,500 of 3,178 sold in 1901, and 2,750 of 7,753 sold in 1902. For the first five years, all Locomobile cars were steam powered, based on designs purchased from the Stanley brothers. The company switched to gas-powered engines in 1904 and remained in business through 1927.

Thwarting Monopolies

Several attempts were made to consolidate early U.S. carmakers into a trust (monopoly), as was happening at the time with railroads, steel, petroleum, and other important sectors of the economy. Pope had created a bicycle trust by acquiring most of the key U.S. patents covering bicycles. EVC, a holding company, tried to monopolize control of manufacturing electric cars, which in 1900 held 40% of the U.S. market and were especially popular in large cities as taxicabs. EVC had been founded as the Electric Storage Battery Company in 1897 by Isaac L. Rice (1850–1915), a pioneer in developing electric-powered submarines. The carmaking operations were taken over in 1899 by New York politician and businessman William C. Whitney (1841–1904) and Peter A. B. Widener (1834–1915), a Philadelphia businessman who invested in street railway companies. Competition from gas-powered cars forced EVC out of the motor vehicle production business after 1900. However, EVC continued to play a leading role, through the Selden patent, in attempts during the first decade of the 20th century to monopolize the U.S. motor vehicle industry.

The Selden patent was a patent held by George B. Selden (1846–1922), a Rochester, New York, lawyer. In 1879, Selden initiated the process of filing a patent on "a liquid-hydrocarbon engine of the compression type" for use in a four-wheeled vehicle. Selden is said to have been inspired to construct a small internal combustion engine after seeing a large one made by George Brayton (1830–1892) at the 1876 Centennial Exposition in Philadelphia. Whether he had actually installed the engine in a vehicle is disputed by automotive historians.

Selden used legal tactics to delay the implementation of the patent for 16 years. Each year, he filed a minor amendment to the patent application, thereby requiring the U.S. Patent Office to conduct a fresh review. By doing this, Selden maintained his claim but put off the start of the 17 year period of exclusive rights granted by a patent. Finally, in 1895, when commercial production of motor vehicles for sale to the public was about to start, Selden was issued patent number 549,160. Thus, at the dawn of the motor vehicle age, George Selden held the sole legal right to sell a motor vehicle, even though he never did so himself.

Holding a valuable patent but lacking the resources to enforce it, Selden sold the rights to the patent in 1899 to EVC, which in turn initiated suits for patent infringement against leading carmakers. In retaliation, several carmakers organized the Manufacturers Mutual Association in 1902, renamed a year later the Association of Licensed Automobile Manufacturers (ALAM). ALAM and EVC negotiated a settlement in 1903 to jointly enforce the Selden patent.

ALAM leased to its members the right to manufacture and sell cars under the Selden patent; within a year, 32 carmakers joined. ALAM licensees paid a fee of 1.25% of the retail price of every gasoline-powered car they sold; ALAM kept 0.5% and turned over 0.75 % to EVC. ALAM ran advertisements threatening not only carmakers that had not paid license fees but also dealers and consumers. For example, one advertisement stated "any person making, selling or using such machines [gasoline-powered cars] made or sold by any unlicensed manufacturers or importers will be liable to prosecution for infringement."[2]

Henry Ford applied for an ALAM license in 1903, but he was turned down on the grounds that he had not yet constructed an operable gasoline engine. Vowing revenge, Ford fought the monopoly with provocative advertisements challenging the legitimacy of the patent. Calling Ford's bluff, ALAM sued him for patent infringement. In 1909, the U.S. District Court upheld the Selden patent, concluding that patent 549,160 did indeed bring together the essential elements of a gasoline-powered car. Several companies, including General Motors, then agreed to pay ALAM royalties of 0.8% on every vehicle they had produced since 1903. Henry Ford refused to pay royalties, pending an appeal, but he placed $12 million in an escrow account to cover eventual payments to ALAM. To calm jittery sellers and buyers of Ford cars, Ford arranged a $6 million bond with the National Casualty Company to cover the potential legal liability of every dealer and owner of Ford cars.

In 1911, the U.S. Court of Appeals reversed the District Court decision. The Selden patent was found valid for vehicles powered by a Brayton-type two-stroke engine. But because nearly all motor vehicles were powered by an Otto-type four-stroke engine, the decision rendered the Selden patent worthless as it applied to motor vehicles. As the patent's seventeen-year enforcement period was due to expire in 1912 anyway, ALAM did not appeal the decision to the U.S. Supreme Court, and the organization dissolved. ALAM's technical efforts were taken over by the Society of Automobile (changed in 1917 to Automotive) Engineers (SAE), which had been founded in 1905 to promote technical standardization among the hundreds of carmakers in the early years of the industry. A century later, SAE continues to be the principal organization promoting technical standards in the industry. The demise of the Selden patent freed the U.S. auto industry from monopolistic licensing practices.

Clustering in Southeastern Michigan

Most histories of the auto industry assert that southeastern Michigan became the industry's home early in the 20th century by accident. For example, John B. Rae says:

> With due allowance for the influence of economic and geographic factors, Detroit became the capital of the automotive kingdom because it happened to possess a unique group of individuals with both business and technical ability who became interested in the possibilities of the motor vehicle.[3]

In reality, although southeastern Michigan was home to talented inventors, a clustering of inventive genius does not spring in isolation from the local industrial climate. The distinctive features of doing business in southeastern Michigan encouraged motor vehicle producers to operate there during the industry's formative years. According to the 1904 U.S. Census of Manufactures, the first to break out carmakers, 42% of all U.S. cars were assembled in Michigan.

Southeastern Michigan attracted or retained the most successful carmakers because the mechanics and engineers most skilled in the key operations for motor vehicle production were already clustered in the region. In particular, skilled operations had to be found for three essential components—an engine to propel the vehicle, a drivetrain to convert engine power to motion, and a chassis strong enough to hold both passengers and the power source. These problems were solved largely through operations borrowed from industries already in southeastern Michigan.

In 1900, only 22% of the roughly 4,000 vehicles sold in the United States had gasoline engines. Steam powered 40% of the vehicles, and electricity 38%. In the 20th century, though, the competition quickly ended: gasoline engines accounted for 83% of sales in 1905, compared to only 12% steam and 5% electricity. Steam-powered cars were easier to manufacture than gasoline-powered cars, and they cost about the same to operate. But steam quickly reached a technological dead-end after 1901, delivering a much less favorable ratio of horsepower to engine weight than gasoline.

Cars with electric engines were especially popular in the large northeastern urban areas, such as New York and Philadelphia, where they were used for deliveries and as taxis. They were quieter and cleaner than the competitors, and easier to operate especially for women. But electric cars were unsuitable outside big cities as they were not powerful enough to traverse unpaved rural roads and had to be recharged every 30 kilometers or so. And the cost of electricity made their cost per distance more than double the cost of cars with other power sources. Had electricity emerged as the dominant source of power, U.S. automotive manufacturing may have clustered in the Northeast instead of the Midwest.

Prior to their adaptation for motor vehicles, gasoline-powered engines were being sold in 1900 primarily for two other purposes. First, small stationery engines were used to generate intermittent power for farm implements and industrial machines in rural settings that lacked access to the urban-centered electricity grid. The leading producer of stationery gas engines was Ransom E. Olds (1864–1950), who set up the first car assembly plant in Detroit in 1901. Second, gasoline engines were also used to power boats. The leading producer of marine engines, Detroit-based Leland & Faulconer, founded in 1890, became a major supplier of car engines and gained a reputation for making precision castings. Its co-founder Henry M. Leland (1843–1932) went on to be president of the Cadillac and the Lincoln car companies.

In addition to Leland & Faulconer, the other leading Detroit-area parts supplier to early carmakers was Dodge Brothers. Dodge made most of the parts for Ford's first cars in 1903, including engines, transmissions, axles, and frames. John Dodge (1864–1920) and Horace Dodge (1868–1920) established a machine shop in Detroit in 1900 to make parts for steam engines and bicycles. They became the first machine shop to concentrate on manufacturing automotive parts in 1901, when Olds gave them a contract. In 1903, Ford ordered engines, transmissions, and axles from the Dodge Brothers, but lacking sufficient cash, paid for the first order largely in shares of the company. Dodge remained Ford's most important supplier until 1914 when Dodge terminated the relationship and two years later began to produce its own cars.

Flint was the center for wagon and carriage production in the United States in 1900. The nation's largest producer of carriages at the time was Durant-Dort Carriage Co. The company was organized in 1886 as the Flint Road Car Co. by William C. Durant (1861–1947), a local entre-preneur, and J. Dallas Dort, manager of a hardware store. Carriage-makers clustered in Flint to take advantage of its proximity to Michigan's extensive hardwood forests. Durant's grandfather Henry Howland Crapo (1804–1869) acquired control over 5,000 hectares of pine forests east of Flint. The timber was cut and floated down the Flint River to Crapo's Flint saw mills. Crapo was elected mayor of Flint in 1860 and gover-nor of Michigan in 1864. Durant built his carriage company into the nation's largest through vertical integration. At a time when carriages sold by competing companies were made under contract with independent manufacturers, Durant-Dort established subsidiaries to manufacture car-riage bodies, wheels, axles, upholstery, springs, varnish, and whip sockets.

Southeastern Michigan also became the center of auto production because of the availability of venture capital, much like Silicon Valley a century later. Carmaking has always been capital intensive. The large assembly plant, the multitude of specialized tools and machinery, the thousands of parts—acquiring all of these assets took a lot of capital a century ago. It is still the case, as robots replace humans for many of the assembly operations, and R&D initiatives become more elaborate.

In 1900, the principal source of financing for industrial development was the large banks clustered in New York City and other northeastern cities. Given that the northeast was also the center of the market for cars in 1900, carmakers naturally looked to that part of the country for capital and factories. However, eastern bankers would not provide adequate financing to the infant car industry. The auto industry was considered too risky.

Turned away by the banks, carmakers turned to sources of capital in Michigan. The leading auto industry venture capitalists proved to be Michigan-based speculators rather than banks. In 1900, much of Michigan's wealth had been produced in three resource-based industries—copper, iron, and lumber. Copper was discovered in Michigan's Upper Peninsula in 1847, and until the late 1880s the state was the world's leading producer. Detroit became the largest producer of iron ships and a national center for other iron products. Michigan's extensive hardwood forests provided lumber for carriage makers. Auto industry pioneers found that people who had made their fortunes in these and related industries in the 20th century were looking for new investment opportunities in the new century. These investors were known as the Princes of Griswold Street, the street where Detroit's financial institutions were clustered.

After failing to obtain financing in New York, Olds' assembly operations were underwritten by Samuel L. Smith, who had made a fortune investing in Michigan's copper and lumber industries through the Michigan Land and Lumber Co. Smith, like Olds, was a Lansing native. Smith became the principal investor in the Olds Motor Works Co in 1899, holding 99.8% of the shares. He became President and his son Fred secretary and treasurer of the Olds Motor Works Co.

Henry Ford also secured capital from wealthy Michigan individuals rather than from banks. Backers of Ford's first venture in 1899 included

William Maybury (1848–1909) and William H. Murphy, who had made fortunes in real estate. Maybury was also Mayor of Detroit. Ford's second attempt at starting a car company was financed by Murphy and James and Hugh McMillan, who controlled the Detroit Dry Dock Co where Ford had once worked. After two failures, even most Detroit financiers shunned Ford. For his third venture—the one that succeeded—Ford secured most of his funds from Alexander Y. Malcomson (1865–1923), a coal merchant. Meanwhile, Murphy took control of the second failed Ford company in 1902. He brought in Henry Leland to run the firm, which was renamed the Cadillac Automobile Company.

CHAPTER 3

Organization of the Motor Vehicle Industry: Production

This chapter focuses on the organization of production of the world's motor vehicles. The next chapter focuses on the organization of vehicle sales. This chapter identifies the leading carmakers and the location of production.

Worldwide production of motor vehicles has increased steadily during the seven decades since the end of World War II at an average annual rate of 1.4% (Figure 3.1). Production increased from 10 million vehicles in 1950 to 16 million in 1960, 30 million in 1970, 39 million in 1980, 44 million in 1990, 58 million in 2000, and 78 million in 2010. The annual average increase was 3.5% during the 1950s, 4.5% during the 1960s, 2.3% during the 1970s, 1.2% during the 1980s, 2.4% during the 1990s, and 1.8% during the first decade of the 21st century.

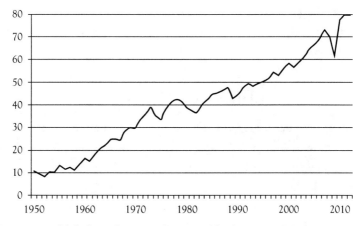

Figure 3.1 Global production of motor vehicles, 1950–2012

Source: U.S. Department of Transportation, Bureau of Transportation Statistics.

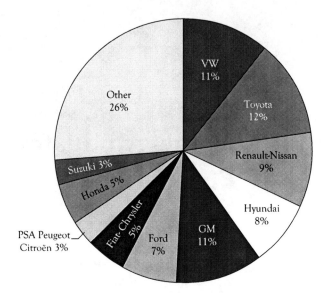

Figure 3.2 Motor vehicle production by company, 2012

Source: Created by author from data compiled by *Automotive News*.

Production increased relatively slowly during the first years of the 1950s before widespread ownership of motor vehicles had diffused through most of the world. Production also stagnated between the mid-1970s and early 1980s, when demand was depressed by escalating petroleum prices. Between 1983 and 2007, production increased relatively rapidly, with declines in only four of those 25 years. Production declined sharply during the severe recession of 2007–2008 but quickly recovered to the historically high levels of volume and growth characteristic of the preceding quarter-century.

The Major Carmakers

Ten carmakers accounted for 76% of the global production of vehicles in 2012 (Figure 3.2). Six of the ten companies assembled between 5 and 10 million vehicles per year each, and the other 4 between 2 million and 5 million. Eight other companies assembled at least 1 million vehicles in 2012, and 21 others produced between 100,000 and 1 million. The six companies that produced at least 5 million vehicles each included two with headquarters in the United States (Ford and General Motors), two in Asia (Hyundai and Toyota), and two in Europe (Renault controlling

Asia-based Nissan and Volkswagen). The other four top producing companies included two in Europe (Fiat controlling U.S.-based Chrysler and PSA Peugeot Citroën) and two in Asia (Honda and Suzuki). These 10 companies all produce and sell vehicles in more than one region of the world.

Whether competition has increased or decreased depends on how it is defined. The 10 largest carmakers increased their share of world production from 68% in 1990 to 75% in 2012. However, the share of world production held by the three largest carmakers declined from 36% in 1990 to 34% in 2012. The number of companies in the world producing at least one million vehicles increased from 13 in 1990 to 18 in 2012. Through a turbulent quarter-century of globalization, severe recession, and regional sharps, the lineup of major carmakers has changed remarkably little. Since 1990, the only changes in the list of 10 largest carmakers have been the takeover of two of them (Chrysler and Nissan) by two others on the list (Fiat and Renault) and the addition of Hyundai and Suzuki to fill the positions vacated by the two takeovers.

Why has there been so little movement in the lineup? On the one hand, very high capital costs are a strong barrier to entry of new large-scale producers. At the same time, the rapid increase in demand worldwide over the past quarter-century, as well as the prospect of strong growth in the future, has encouraged even unprofitable carmakers to stay in business to grab a portion of the additional sales.

The following is a review of the world's 10 largest producers of vehicles, as of 2012, in alphabetical order.

Fiat/Chrysler

Fiat, an acronym for Fabbrica Italiana Automobili Torino, was founded in 1899 under the leadership of Giovanni Agnelli (1866–1945). The Agnelli family has remained in control of Fiat for most of its century-plus existence, either through direct management of the firm or indirectly through a family-owned holding company. Giovanni Agnelli's great-great-grandson John Elkann became chairman in 2010. Fiat emerged early in the 20th century as Italy's leading carmaker, primarily by focusing on high-volume, mass-produced, low-priced cars. High tariffs and trade barriers protected Fiat in its home market.

The Agnelli family has played an extremely prominent role in Italian politics, culture, and aristocratic society through the 20th century and into the twenty-first.[1] Fiat especially dominates its home city of Turin. In addition to being by far the city's largest employer for more than a century, the Fiat holding company owns the city's principal newspaper *La Stampa* and its leading soccer team Juventus Football Club. The company's iconic factory in the Lingotto district of Turin opened in 1923 and stopped producing cars in 1982, but it was remodeled by the architect Renzo Piano into a complex including a hotel, shopping mall, university, concert hall, and theater as well as corporate offices for Fiat.

Fiat gained control of U.S.-based Chrysler in 2009 as part of that company's U.S. government-managed restructuring. Chrysler Motor Corporation was incorporated in 1924 by Walter Chrysler, who had been president of GM's Buick division during the 1910s. During the early 1920s, Walter Chrysler was hired by banks to reorganize several insolvent carmakers, including Maxwell Motor Company and Chalmers, which were folded into Chrysler. Early Chrysler cars quickly gained a reputation for especially strong engineering. As sales rapidly increased, Chrysler acquired Dodge Brothers in 1926. Dodge had been founded by brothers John and Horace Dodge in 1900 to make car parts. The company grew rapidly because it was a leading supplier to Ford, and the Dodge brothers were major investors in Ford. Dodge started to assemble complete vehicles sold under its own name in 1915. Dodge was the second bestselling car in the United States in 1920, when both the Dodge brothers died. The Dodges' widows sold the company in 1925 to an investment firm Dillon, Read & Co. (currently part of UBS), which in turn sold it to Chrysler three years later.

Chrysler acquired American Motors (AMC) from Renault in 1987. AMC was formed in 1954 through the acquisition of Hudson Motor Car Company by Nash-Kelvinator Corporation. In 1916, Charles P. Nash (1864–1948), a former GM president, acquired the Thomas B. Jeffery Company, a nineteenth-century bicycle manufacturer in Kenosha, Wisconsin, that started to assemble cars in 1902. Hudson had been established in Detroit in 1909 by Roy D. Chapin Sr. (1880–1936); the carmaker was named for its principal financial backer, Joseph L. Hudson (1846–1912), who was also the founder of Detroit's leading department store of the same name.

The principal asset that passed through AMC and Chrysler was the Jeep brand. Jeep originated as a vehicle commissioned by the U.S. Army in 1940 in anticipation of U.S. entry into World War II. The prototype was developed by the American Bantam Car Company, but the Army deemed Bantam too small to meet its needs, so it contracted Willys-Overland Motor Company to produce Jeeps. Willys-Overland made substantial alterations to the prototype and assembled 363,000 Jeeps during World War II. Ford assembled another 280,000 Jeeps during World War II using specifications supplied by Willys-Overland.

Willys-Overland was the second leading carmaker after Ford during the 1910s but had slipped well behind the leaders during the 1930s. John Willys (1873–1935) formed Willys-Overland through acquisition of a number of carmakers during the first two decades of the 20th century, beginning in 1908 with a division of the Standard Wheel Company that had started making cars called Overland in 1903. After World War II, Willys-Overland produced Jeeps for sale to civilians as well as the Army. Willys-Overland, including the Jeep, was purchased by Kaiser Motors in 1953. Kaiser (originally Kaiser-Frazer Corporation), founded in 1945 by Edgar Kaiser and Joseph Frazer, was one of a number of companies that started producing cars in the United States after World War II but ultimately failed during the 1950s. In Kaiser's case, it halted production of cars in 1955 but continued to make Jeeps until 1970, when the company was sold to American Motors.

With European integration, Fiat has been especially aggressive entering Eastern Europe, and its largest European factories are now in Poland. Fiat has also been especially strong in South America with plants in Argentina and Brazil. Fiat's half-dozen assembly plants in Italy now are utilized at very low rates, well under half of capacity.

Ford Motor Company

The Ford Motor Company, established in 1903, was Henry Ford's third attempt to start a car company, after two failures.[2] At a time when cars were luxury recreational toys for the wealthy living in big cities, Ford argued that cars would have practical applications, especially for farmers in rural areas. Most financial backers in the auto industry believed that profits resulted from selling at a high price a small quantity of handmade cars. Ford was convinced that demand for cars would become universal and was limited in 1900 only by the high prices. At odds with his financial backers, Ford set out to build the lowest-priced car possible. When introduced in 1909, the Ford Model T was initially priced at $850 at a time when most cars sold for around $2,000. The price dropped to $440 in 1915 and $260 in the 1920s. More than 15 million Model Ts were sold, the most of any model until passed by the VW Beetle in 1972. During the 1910s, more than half the cars in the entire world, as well as in the United States, were Model Ts.

Henry Ford became a folk hero for paying his workers $5 a day in 1914, more than twice the rate at other factories. He ran for the U.S. Senate from Michigan and narrowly lost in a race that many considered stolen from him. But the Ford Motor Co. failed to keep pace with the improved technology, design, and marketing of GM as well as upstart Chrysler. Henry Ford became increasingly authoritarian and erratic. He published anti-Semitic material, attacked the banking and entertainment industries, and accepted a medal from Nazi Germany. Disdainful of his only son Edsel, who died at a young age, Henry Ford turned over day-to-day management of the company's Service Department to Harry Bennett, a former boxer with known connections to organized crime. The Service Department enforced draconian rules in the factory, beat up union organizers in front of news cameras, and checked up on workers in their homes. During World War II, the U.S. Government came close to nationalizing the troubled company to assure availability of essential war materiel.

In 1919, Henry Ford bought out all minority shareholders and held 100% of the stock of the company. A public stock offering was initiated in 1956, but the Ford family has retained financial control in the company through a special class of stock. The family has also retained control of the company's management. With Henry Ford no longer competent to run the company in his old age, and his only child Edsel deceased, the oldest grandson Henry Ford II took over, serving as President, Chairman, or CEO from 1945 until 1979. To revive the company's fortunes, Henry II hired a strong management team known as the Whiz Kids. The current Executive Chairman of the company, William C. Ford, Jr., is the great-grandson of Henry Ford, as well as of Harvey Firestone, founder of what is today part of the world's largest tire producer. The Ford family plays a leadership role in the Detroit area, including ownership of the Detroit Lions National Football League team.

The Ford Motor Co. survived the severe recession of 2008–2009 without the government intervention and bankruptcy proceedings required to save Chrysler and GM. Credited with Ford's success was a strong leadership team, including Bill Ford and the President and CEO Alan Mulally, who had been hired from Boeing Corp. Assets not central to the company's primary mission of building popularly priced Ford brand models were sold. The company put up nearly all of its remaining assets as collateral to borrow money before the credit markets froze.

Ford pioneered overseas assembly plants. Its first overseas factory—in Trafford Park, a suburb of Manchester, England—opened in 1911 to assemble the Model T, which quickly became the best-selling vehicle in the United Kingdom. Earlier, in 1904, an independent company, the Walkerville Wagon Works, gained the rights to manufacture Ford vehicles in Canada. Ford's principal assembly production facilities in Europe are in Germany, Spain, and Turkey. Ford has had a major presence in Eastern Europe for a long time, including facilities in Romania and Russia. It has closed European assembly plants in Belgium and the United Kingdom. South America markets are served from plants in Argentina, Brazil, and Venezuela. Ford has plants in India, Malaysia, and Vietnam. It is producing in China but trails the other major carmakers in that market. On the other hand, Ford has historically been a leader in production in Australia and South Africa.

General Motors

The story of General Motors differs from that of the other leading carmakers because it was originally designed to be a loosely organized holding company for highly autonomous assemblers and parts suppliers rather than a single tightly integrated manufacturing enterprise. GM's founder William C. Durant incorporated GM in Flint, Michigan, in 1908 to oversee a number of companies he had acquired.[3] Most of Durant's acquisitions were manufacturers of obscure but necessary car parts or insolvent small-scale vehicle assemblers. Durant had founded and run the Flint-based Durant-Dort Carriage Company, which by 1900 had become the largest carriage manufacturer in the United States.

The strongest performing carmaker in the original GM was Buick. In 1904, Durant had acquired a then-struggling Buick Motor Company, which was also based in Flint and turned it into the world's best-selling brand in 1909.

Ousted from GM in 1910 by bankers unhappy with the company's mounting financial losses, Durant formed two more auto companies, named Republic Motors and United Motors. He repeated his earlier strategy of acquiring obscure parts suppliers and insolvent assemblers, including Chevrolet Motor Company. Durant regained control of GM in 1916 and combined his various holdings into a company that was large enough to challenge Ford as the world's largest carmaker. With GM once again financially overextended, Durant was forced out of the company for a second and final time in 1920. GM was taken over by E. I. du Pont de Nemours and Company (DuPont), which saw it as a lucrative customer for its paint products. GM passed Ford for good in 1931 as the best-selling vehicle producer in the United States, a title it has never relinquished. It was the world's best-selling carmaker from the 1920s until overtaken by Toyota in 2008. Its principal overseas acquisitions were the United Kingdom's Vauxhall Motors in 1925 and Germany's Opel in 1929.

Alfred P. Sloan, the owner of one of the many parts companies acquired by Durant, was installed as GM President in 1923. He continued as President or Chairman of the Board until 1956. Under Sloan, GM became not only the world's largest carmaker but, for a number of years, the world's larger corporation of any sort. GM was considered a model of how a very large corporation could be successfully operated through decentralization and vertical integration. Each GM division had to meet a specified rate of return on investment but had considerable leeway in how to achieve it. GM was especially adept for much of the 20th century at marketing a variety of cars at various price points and styles, from the low-priced, mass-market Chevrolet to the exclusive, expensive Cadillac. For many years, as GM held roughly half of the North American market, one of its brands would regard other GM brands, rather than other carmakers, as its chief competitors.

GM's market share in the United States started slipping, dropping from a historic high of 50 percent in 1956 to below 40% in 1986, below 30% in 1998, and below 20% in 2010. The long-term slippage in market share was somewhat masked by steady sales in the range of 4–5 million vehicles per year during the 1980s, 1990s, and most of the 2000s, although still below its historic U.S. high of 6.9 million in 1978. GM continued to operate as if nothing were amiss and its sales and market share would rebound to historic levels. Finally, during the severe recession of 2008–2009, as its sales plummeted from 3.8 million in 2007 to 2 million in 2009, GM ran out of cash. It asked the U.S. Government for help, and President Obama's Auto Task Force responded by replacing GM's top leadership and restructuring the company through bankruptcy laws. The government-managed restructuring turned GM into a smaller, financially viable company with its toxic assets isolated from the viable on-going business. GM has continued to lose market share in the United States but has been profitable at its smaller size. A large proportion of its facilities were closed as part of the government-managed restructuring.

Outside North America, GM's production facilities are distributed in a pattern similar to Ford's. Like Ford, GM has its principal European assembly plants in Germany and Spain, and like Ford, it has closed plants in Belgium and the United Kingdom. Eastern Europe is served primarily from plants in Poland. In Asia, in addition to China and India, GM is assembling vehicles in Thailand and Vietnam. Like Ford, GM has its major South American facilities in Brazil and also in Venezuela. Again like Ford, GM has a major presence in Australia and South America.

Honda Motor Company

Honda Motor Company was founded by Soichiro Honda. Prior to World War II, he ran a car repair shop and, in 1937, organized Tokai Seiki Heavy Industry to make piston rings for Toyota. Honda started making motorcycles in 1948 and has been the world's largest motorcycle producer since 1959. Motorcycles now represent only 14% of the company's revenues. Honda first produced motor vehicles in 1963.

Honda's corporate strategy is distinctive among the largest carmakers in two ways. First, the company has chosen to focus to a greater degree than its North American competitors on passenger cars rather than trucks. Unlike the other major carmakers in North America, Honda does not produce large pickup trucks. Honda has depended instead on two high-volume passenger cars, Accord and Civic, and numerous other vehicles based on the platforms of these two vehicles. As a result, Honda's market position is stronger when demand for trucks is weaker and its market position is poorer when demand for trucks is higher.

Honda's second distinctive position is its large share of sales in North America. An also-ran with a relatively small market share and limited growth prospects in its home market in Japan, Honda became one of the world's largest carmakers by becoming the first Japanese-owned company to assemble vehicles in North America, beginning in Marysville, Ohio, in 1982.[4] It continued its leadership as the first Japanese-owned carmaker to build a second assembly plant in North America, in East Liberty, Ohio. Although its headquarters are in Japan, Honda gets nearly half of its sales in North America compared to only one-sixth in Japan. In comparison, one-third of Toyota's worldwide sales are in North America and one-fourth in Japan. Ultimately, success abroad translated into growth in its home market, as Honda passed Nissan in 2001 to be the second leading producer of vehicles in Japan.

Honda is a leading producer in South and Southeast Asia with assembly plants in India, Indonesia, New Zealand, Pakistan, and Thailand. In South America, Honda has plants in Argentina and Brazil. The European market is served from plants in Turkey and the United Kingdom.

Soichiro Honda remained head of the company until 1973 and was active in the company until his death in 1991. Since then, the company has been owned by individual and corporate shareholders, without Honda family involvement. The largest shareholder, with 7% of shares, is the Japan Trustee Services Bank.

Hyundai Motor Group

Hyundai is the newcomer and fastest growing among the top 10 carmakers. The other leading carmakers trace their roots to the 19th or early 20th centuries, but Hyundai only began making cars in 1967, originally assembling Ford cars for the Korean market. The first Hyundai-designed car was not built until 1974. It did not start selling vehicles in the United States until 1986 and opened its first U.S. plant in 2005.

Hyundai Motor Group was organized in 1998 through the combination of South Korea's two leading carmakers Hyundai Motors and Kia Motors. In 1998, Hyundai was the world's sixteenth largest producer.

After it consolidated with Kia, the combined company jumped to thirteenth largest in 1999. The combined company became the world's eleventh largest carmaker in 2000, eighth largest in 2001, seventh largest in 2003, sixth largest in 2009, and fifth largest in 2010. The company's policy has been to become a major international player by offering vehicles regarded by consumers and critics as competitive in quality with, yet less expensive than, the leading Japanese makes.

Hyundai Motors is part of South Korea's largest *chaebol* (conglomerate), which was formed in 1947, starting with a construction firm. Chung Ju-yung (1915–2001) controlled the Hyundai *chaebol* until his death in 2001. The *chaebol* were created in Korea to help foster rapid and economic development and industrialization. The *chaebol* have centralized ownership, primarily the families that founded it. Some are involved in a large variety of activities, but most focus on core competences.

The original Hyundai *chaebol,* broken up around 2000, continues primarily as a shipping company. Most companies bearing the Hyundai name are now separate legal entities from Hyundai Motor Group, including Hyundai department store, heavy industries, and development companies. Hyundai Motor Group includes several so-called affiliated companies in addition to the carmaking Hyundai Motors. Affiliations include steel, car parts, construction, logistics, finance, and IT companies.

Kia, which became part of the Hyundai Motor Group in 1998, had been founded in 1944 to make bicycle parts. Kia started building cars in 1974 and became South Korea's second-largest carmaker. Its products were derived primarily from Mazda, which was controlled at the time by Ford. Kia declared bankruptcy in 1997, and Hyundai outbid Ford for controlling interest.

The home country accounts for a smaller share of Hyundai's total worldwide sales than any other major carmaker, not surprising given the relatively small size of the Korean market. China, the United States, and South Korea each account for around one-sixth of the company's global sales. Hyundai is producing for the South American market in Brazil and for the European market in the Czech Republic, Russia, and Turkey. Like the other major carmakers, Hyundai has a presence in China and India.

PSA Peugeot Citroën

PSA Peugeot Citroën is the oldest of the world's 10 largest carmakers.[5] A metalworking firm, Peugeot Frères Aînés built its first gasoline-powered cars in 1890 under license from Gottlieb Daimler, who had patented a gasoline engine only five years earlier. The company was originally founded in 1810 to manufacture coffee mills, and it started to make bicycles in 1830. Cousins Armand and Eugène Peugeot split in 1896, with Armand establishing Société Anonyme des Automobiles Peugeot to focus on making cars and Eugène remaining in charge of the long-standing family metalworking business. The two Peugeot companies merged in 1910.

PSA was formed in 1976 amidst a buying spree by Peugeot S.A. during a period of consolidation in the wake of economic hardships brought on by the oil shocks. Peugeot acquired a 38.2% share of Citroën in 1974 and raised it to 89.9% in 1976. PSA also acquired Chrysler Europe in 1978.

André-Gustave Citroën (1878–1935) started building cars in 1919 in a factory he originally opened to produce armaments for the French government during World War I. The company filed for bankruptcy in 1934, and its assets were taken over by the company's largest creditor Michelin. During World War II, Citroën was notable for cooperating less with the German occupiers and providing more active support to the resistance than did other French companies, in part a legacy of André Citroën being Jewish.

After World War II, Citroën's fortunes were temporarily revived by streamlined designs, especially two unusually innovative and iconic models, the 2CV (deux chevaux) economy car and the DS with pneumatic suspension. The company bought the French pioneering carmaker Panhard in 1965 but two years later terminated the Panhard nameplate. Fiat acquired a 49% share of Michelin and thus of Citroën in 1968 but sold the shares back to Michelin five years later. A year later Citroën filed for bankruptcy protection, and the French government arranged for Michelin to sell its shares in Citroën to Peugeot. Peugeot and Citroën have separate marketing operations but share R&D and assembly operations.

Peugeot acquired Chrysler Europe in 1978 for $1 plus assumption of its liabilities and properties. Attempting to compete with Ford and GM as a major player in Europe, Chrysler Corporation acquired several long-standing European carmakers and operated them under the umbrella of Chrysler Europe.

- Rootes Group was founded in 1913 by William Rootes (1894–1964) and became the largest carmaker in the United Kingdom through acquisition of several companies, including Hillman and Humber in 1929 and Talbot and Sunbeam in 1935. After Lord Rootes's death, the company was taken over by Chrysler, which over a period of years replaced the long-standing brand names with Chrysler. After acquiring Chrysler Europe, Peugeot revived the Talbot nameplate for eight years before renaming the models Peugeots.
- Simca, an acronym for Société Industrielle de Mécanique et Carrosserie Automobile (Industrial Society of Mechanical and Automotive Body), was founded in 1934 by Fiat to produce vehicles in France. A Fiat executive, Henri Théodore Pigozzi (who changed his name from the Italian Enrico Teodoro), ran Simca from 1935 until 1963, when Chrysler bought Fiat's controlling interest. Simca had acquired Ford's France operations in 1958 and utilized a former Ford facility as its principal assembly plant.
- Barreiros, founded in 1954 by Eduardo Barreiros to produce diesel engines and trucks, started to produce Chrysler cars for the Spanish market in 1963. Chrysler took full control of the company in 1969.

Renault/Nissan

Louis Renault (1877–1944) built his first car in 1898, in a workshop, which has been preserved, along the banks of the River Seine about 2 kilometers west of Paris in the commune of Boulogne-Billancourt. Louis founded Société Renault Frères in 1899 along with brothers Marcel and Fernand. Renault's corporate headquarters remain along the banks of the Seine.

In 1919, Louis Renault purchased the entire Île Seguin, a 1-kilometer-long, 15-hectare island in the Seine opposite his workshop. A decade later, he started construction of a large factory complex on the island. Boulogne-Billancourt, as the island complex was known, was France's largest factory with 30,000 employees, Renault's only manufacturing facility prior to World War II, and its largest facility until its closure in 1992. Heavy Allied bombing heavily damaged the complex during World War II, preventing it from being used to supply the Nazi army. Nearly all of the structures on Île Seguin were demolished between 2000 and 2002. Plans for a museum on the island fell through; a restaurant and park are now there. Renault's headquarters are located along the banks of the Seine facing the island.

After the liberation of France in 1944, Louis Renault was arrested on charges of collaborating with the Nazis, and he died in jail later that year. The French government nationalized the carmaker in 1945. Appointed as the first chairman of the nationalized carmaker was Pierre Lefaucheux (1898–1955), a leader of the French Resistance during World War II and a concentration camp survivor. Lefaucheux set a style of management at Renault that minimized the impact of being nationalized. Resisting political pressure to focus on truck production, Lefaucheux's priority was building small cars that became the best-selling models in France. Renault was privatized in 1996, although the French government continues to own around 15%.

Nissan Motor Company's predecessor, originally called the Kwaishinsha Motor Car Works, was founded in 1911 by Masujiro Hashimoto. The company sold cars named DAT, derived from the acronym of the three major investors Kenjiro Den, Rokuro Aoyama, and Meitaro Takeuchi, and the company's name was changed in 1925 to DAT Motorcar Company. DAT was acquired in 1930 by Nippon Sangyo, one of Japan's largest holding companies. The carmaker was set up as a separate subsidiary Nissan Motor in 1934. The name Nissan came from the abbreviation used on the Tokyo Stock Exchange for Nippon Sangyo. Renault acquired controlling interest in Nissan in 1999; Renault's CEO Carlos Ghosn took on the same title at Nissan. Renault owned 44% of Nissan as of 2013 and Nissan 15% of Renault. Renault also owns these formerly independent carmakers:

- Dacia, established in 1966, was Romania's leading carmaker, producing vehicles primarily derived from Renault designs and tooling. Renault acquired Dacia in 1999 and has used the

nameplate for lower priced models sold primarily in Eastern
Europe.

- AvtoVAZ, founded in 1966 as Volzhsky Avtomobilny Zavod
  (VAZ), was Russia's leading carmaker, producing vehicles
  based primarily on Fiat models and sold under the Lada
  nameplate. Renault-Nissan took majority control in 2012.
- Samsung Motors, established in South Korea in 1994 by one
  of the country's leading firms, was sold to Renault in 2000.
- Oyak was founded in Turkey in 1969 as a joint venture
  between Renault, which owns 51%, and the Turkish Armed
  Forces Pension Fund, which owns 49%.

Suzuki Motor Corporation

Suzuki Loom Works was established by Michio Suzuki (1887–1982) in
1909 to manufacture looms for the silk industry and later for cotton.
Efforts initiated during the 1930s to build motor vehicles were shelved
with the outbreak of World War II. After the war, Suzuki—like Honda—
entered the motor industry first with two-wheeled vehicles, beginning
with motorized bicycles in 1952, then motorcycles, then cars in 1955.
The company has specialized in small cars and trucks, and its fortunes
have ebbed and flowed with the changing demand for small cars in Japan
and elsewhere.

Suzuki formed joint ventures in 1981 with GM and Japanese truck
producer Isuzu to build small cars and trucks for the North American
market. Suzuki has also been a partner in developing vehicles with an
unusually large number of other carmakers. The purpose of the joint ventures is to make full use of assembly plants by producing vehicles that are
sold under the nameplates of more than one carmaker. GM owned more
than 20% of Suzuki at the peak of the partnership between 2001 and
2006, but GM sold 17% in 2006 and the remainder two years later. VW
now owns 20% of the company and is the largest shareholder. Relations
between VW and Suzuki have been turbulent.

Suzuki's most important subsidiary is Maruti, which has long been
India's leading carmaker. Maruti Technical Services Limited was formed
in 1970 by the Government of India for the purpose of developing and

mass-producing a low-priced car. Although lacking experience in the auto industry, Sanjay Gandhi—son of then Prime Minister Indira Gandhi—was awarded an exclusive license to produce Maruti cars. The company was liquidated following a scandal in 1977, and Sanjay Gandhi died in a plane crash in 1980.

The company was re-established in 1981 as Maruti Udyog [Hindi for "industry"]. When it finally started producing cars in 1983, Suzuki provided the designs and operated the company as a joint venture with the Indian government. With economic liberalization during the 1990s, the Indian government permitted Suzuki to acquire one-half of Maruti in 1992 and finally a controlling 54% in 2002.

As a specialist in producing relatively inexpensive small cars and trucks, Suzuki is a major player in the emerging markets of Asia. In addition to India, Suzuki has production facilities in Indonesia, Myanmar, Pakistan, and the Philippines. It also produces for Europe through an assembly plant in one of that region's emerging markets, Hungary. Meanwhile, Suzuki's U.S. subsidiary filed for bankruptcy in 2012 and stopped selling in the U.S. market.

Toyota Motor Company

Toyota, like Suzuki, traces its corporate roots to the textile industry.[6] Toyoda Automatic Loom Company, founded by Sakichi Toyoda in 1924 to manufacture weaving machinery, established a carmaking division in 1933 under the leadership of Sakichi's son Kiichiro. Toyota Motor Corporation became an independent company in 1937. The company name was changed from the family name Toyoda to Toyota because the spelling with the "t" is regarded as carrying good fortune in Japanese, whereas the spelling with the "d" means "fertile rice paddies."

The Toyoda family has dominated the management of the carmaker. The founder Kiichiro Toyoda was president of the carmaker until 1950. His son Shoichiro was president during 1982–1992, and Shoichiro's son Akio became president and CEO in 2009. The family owns 9% of the company, although its stake is smaller than those held by the Ford, Peugeot, and Agnelli [Fiat] families in their respective carmakers. The largest stakeholder, holding 10% of the shares, is Japan Trustee Services

Bank, two-thirds of which is owned by Sumitomo Mitsui Trust Holdings and one-third by Resona Bank. Both of these financial institutions have substantial backing from the Japanese government.

Nissan was Japan's oldest and leading carmaker prior to World War II, but as Japanese carmakers restructured in the decade after the country's defeat, Toyota passed Nissan to become by far Japan's best-selling carmaker without exception through the second half of the 20th century and into the 21st.

Toyota controls two other Japanese vehicle manufacturers—Daihatsu Motor Co. and Hino Motors. Daihatsu (known until 1951 as Hatsudoki Seizo Co. Ltd) was Japan's oldest carmaker, founded in 1907. The company specialized in smaller cars and exports to developing countries. Toyota acquired a controlling 51% interest in 1999. Hino was founded in 1917 by Tokyo Gas Industry Company, which had been established seven years earlier to produce gas and electric parts. Since becoming part of Toyota in 1967, the company has focused on production of medium- and heavy-duty trucks.

Toyota also owns 17% of Fuji Heavy Industries, which produces Subaru cars. Fuji was founded in 1915 to produce aircraft. It started assembling cars in 1954. Nissan acquired 20% of Fuji's shares in 1968. When Renault acquired control of Nissan in 1999, the Fuji shares were sold to GM. GM in turn sold 9% of Fuji's shares to Toyota in 2005 and sold the rest of its 20% stake to the public.

Toyota supplies the European market through facilities in France, Portugal, and the United Kingdom. South American facilities are in Argentina and Brazil. Indonesia and Thailand are sites of major production facilities in Southeast Asia. As with other major carmakers, Toyota has facilities in Australia and South Africa.

Volkswagen GmbH

Volkswagen GmbH (known in its first year as Gesellschaft zur Vorbereitung des Deutschen Volkswagens mbH) was founded in 1937 by the Deutsche Arbeitsfront, the National Socialist union established by the Nazis.[7] The purpose of the company was to build a low-priced car that would be affordable for a large percentage of Germans. A factory was constructed in Wolfsburg (known before World War II as KdF-Stadt) in 1938, but only a few cars were produced before the factory was converted to military vehicles with the outbreak of World War II in 1939.

After World War II, Wolfsburg—including the VW factory—was in the British occupied sector. The British military tried but failed to find an international carmaker willing to take over the VW factory, though Ford strongly considered it. Instead, the company was restructured in 1949 under the ownership of the Federal Republic of Germany. The government sold its shares in 1960.

VW concentrated on building a single model, a beetle-shaped car that passed the Model T in 1972 as the world's best-selling model of all time. A year later, production of the beetle ended in Europe, but it continued in Mexico until 2003. Ultimately, 21.5 million cars were produced worldwide.

VW took over several smaller German companies during the 1960s. Auto Union, acquired in 1964, had been formed in 1932 by consolidating four small German carmakers Audi, DKW, Horch, and Wandered, all originally founded between 1904 and 1916. NSU, acquired in 1969 and folded into Auto Union, was originally a manufacturer of knitting machines and had started to make cars in 1905.

VW solidified its position as the best-selling carmaker in Europe by acquiring SEAT and Škoda. Škoda began as a manufacturer of armaments in 1859 and motorcycles in 1898, adding cars in 1905. The company was nationalized after the communist takeover of Czechoslovakia in 1948. After the fall of communism in 1989, Škoda was auctioned off by the government, and VW outbid Renault for it.

SEAT (an acronym for Sociedad Española de Automóviles de Turismo, or Spanish Touring Car Company) was founded in 1950 by the government of Spain. The company became the dominant carmaker in Spain, producing primarily vehicles derived from an alliance with Fiat. SEAT switched its alliance in 1982 to VW, which acquired 51% of the company in 1986. In 1990, SEAT became a wholly owned subsidiary of VW.

VW also owns the premium carmaker Porsche through a complex series of arrangements designed to ward off a hostile takeover of VW. Ferdinand Porsche was the designer of the original VW beetle. A Porsche holding company actually owns most of VW, but VW in turn controls the holding company. The State of Lower Saxony owns 20% of VW, and the government of Qatar 17%.

VW has positioned Audi and Porsche as premium brands, Seat and Škoda as low-priced brands, and the Volkswagen division as the high-volume, mid-priced brand. VW accounted for half of the company's sales in Europe in 2012, whereas the other brands divided the remaining half. Outside of Europe, VW also is the leading carmaker in China and Mexico.

Distribution of Vehicle Production

Vehicle production in 2012 exceeded 1 million in seventeen countries, including seven in Asia, five in Europe, three in North America, one in Latin America, and Russia. Another twenty countries had production in excess of 100,000, including 10 in Europe, six in Asia, and two each in Africa and Latin America.

Three regions—Asia, Europe, and North America—account for 94% of the world's motor vehicle production. In 2012, 44 million vehicles were produced in Asia (including Oceania), 20 million in Europe (including Russia), 16 million in North America (including Mexico), 4 million in South America, and 1 million in Africa and the Middle East. Thus, more than one-half of the world's vehicles were assembled in Asia, nearly one-fourth in Europe, and nearly one-fifth in North America (Figure 3.3).

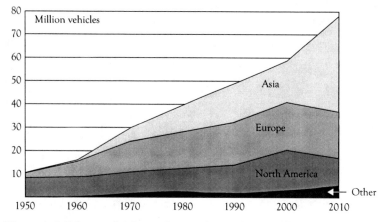

Figure 3.3 Motor vehicle production by world region, 1950–2012

Source: U.S. Department of Transportation, Bureau of Transportation Statistics.

Within each of the three regions of motor vehicle production, assembly plants have distinctive distributions.[8]

Distribution of Production Within North America

In 1950, 8 million of the world's 10 million vehicles were produced in just one country, the United States. U.S. dominance of world production dated from Ford's installation of the moving assembly line and adoption of other elements of mass production during the 1910s. Other industrialized countries had not fully recovered from the devastation of World War II by 1950, and industrialization had not yet diffused to other regions.

The U.S. motor vehicle industry consolidated in the hands of three companies—GM, Ford, and Chrysler—known for much of the 20th century as "the Big Three." By the 1950s, the Big Three together accounted for 95% of car production and sales in the United States. In the 21st century, GM, Ford, and Chrysler produce only half of the vehicles in North America, and reflecting their less dominant position, they are now known as the Detroit Three rather than the Big Three. Japanese carmakers constructed assembly plants in North America beginning with Honda in 1982, and foreign-headquartered companies now account for half of the vehicles produced in North America.

The North American auto industry is highly clustered in a region known as auto alley (Figure 3.4).[9] Auto alley is a narrow corridor approximately 100 kilometers wide and 1,000 kilometers long that extends north–south between the Great Lakes and the Gulf of Mexico. The spine of auto alley through the United States is formed by two north-south interstate highways, I-65 and I-75. East-west highways, including I-40, I-64, I-70, and US 30, form ladders connecting the two north-south routes. Auto alley extends into southwestern Ontario along Highway 401. The principal auto production center in North America outside of auto alley is in Mexico.

U.S. motor vehicle production clustered in southeastern Michigan during the first decade of the 20th century. Until then, production had been scattered across the northeast. Carmakers clustered in southeastern Michigan primarily because of proximity to key inputs. The leading manufacturers of gasoline engines, transmissions, and carriage bodies were in

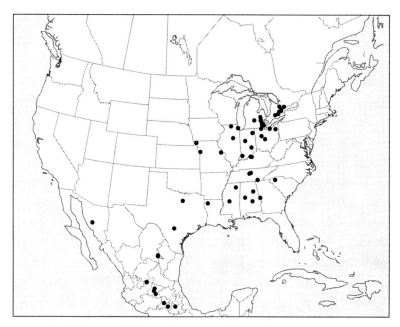

Figure 3.4 Motor vehicle production in North America

Source: Compiled by author and Thomas Klier, Senior Economist, Federal Reserve Bank of Chicago, from data published by Ward's *Automotive* and *Automotive News*.

the region. In addition, wealthy investors in the Detroit area were willing to provide capital for fledgling carmakers at a time when the industry was viewed as an unacceptable risk by leading banks in New York and elsewhere in the northeast.

The emergence of the Ford Motor Co. as the dominant carmaker in the second decade of the 20th century signaled a change in the geography of production. Ford produced most of the parts in southeastern Michigan and shipped them to large cities around the country where they were put together into completed vehicles at branch assembly plants. GM, Chrysler, and smaller carmakers emulated Ford's branch assembly plant strategy.

The Detroit Three carmakers closed their branch assembly plants beginning in the 1970s, and all of them were gone in the early 21st century. New assembly plants were constructed and older ones modernized in auto alley in order to minimize aggregate shipping costs to the entire North American market. Meanwhile, when Japanese-owned carmakers began to construct assembly plants in the United States in the 1980s, they also sought locations in auto alley.

Within auto alley, a spatial division has emerged between the north and the south. North of US 30 (Michigan and northern portions of Illinois, Indiana, and Ohio), all 18 assembly plants are owned by the Detroit Three carmakers. To the south, 16 of 18 assembly plants are owned by foreign-headquartered carmakers.

For much of the 20th century, U.S.-owned carmakers produced vehicles in Canada for sale in Canada and vehicles in Mexico for sale in Mexico. Trade restrictions limited the number of vehicles produced in one North American country and sold in another. Free trade agreements between the United States and Canada resulted in integration of production between those two countries beginning in the 1960s. The North American Free Trade Agreement extended the integration of production to Mexico beginning in the 1980s.

Mexico is the principal center of vehicle production outside auto alley. Assembly plants within Mexico are located either near Mexico City, the country's largest market, or in the north to minimize shipping to U.S. customers.

Distribution of Production Within Europe

Motor vehicle production increased rapidly in Europe during the 1950s and 1960s, from less than 2 million in 1950 to more than 13 million in 1970. Europe's share of world production reached a historic high of 44% in 1970, before declining to 35% in 2000 and 25% in 2010.

Fifteen of 27 European Union (EU) countries produce at least 100,000 vehicles a year. Germany accounts for about one-third of vehicle production; France and Spain together are responsible for another one-fourth. The United Kingdom ranks fourth among the 27 EU countries.

Vehicle production in Europe originated independently in each country. High tariffs minimized the movement of vehicles among countries within Europe, let alone from other world regions, for most of the 20th century. With most vehicles produced in an individual country also sold in that country, the optimal locations for production were near the geographic center of the various national markets, or near the wealthiest regions where car buyers were most numerous. Thus, most assembly plants in the United Kingdom were located in the West Midlands, especially near the city of Coventry. The Paris region was the center of national production in France, Turin in Italy, and Wolfsburg in Germany.

Although the EU has eliminated barriers to movement of vehicles within Europe, labor laws make it difficult to close assembly plants in Europe. As a result, the distribution of plants within Europe is influenced by the legacy of protected national carmakers. Nevertheless, despite national legacies, the distribution of assembly plants within Europe is highly clustered and occupies an area of approximately the same size as North America's auto alley. Europe's auto producing region is oriented east–west between the United Kingdom and Slovakia. The heart of the region is southern and western Germany, where a high percentage of the continent's production is centered. The other principal production area in Europe is in northern Spain (Figure 3.5).[10]

The fastest growing car producing area within the EU is Eastern Europe. The Czech Republic, Poland, Slovakia, and Romania together

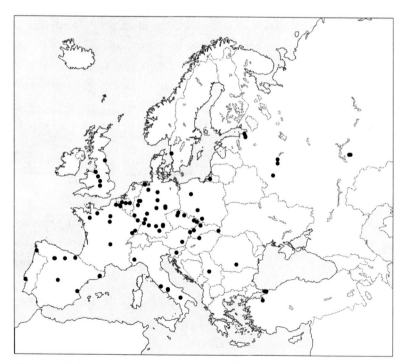

Figure 3.5 Motor vehicle production in Europe

Source: Compiled by author and Thomas Klier, Senior Economist, Federal Reserve Bank of Chicago, from data published by *Ward's Automotive* and *Automotive News.*

accounted for 16% of total EU output in 2012, compared to only 3% in 1970. These former Communist countries have much lower wage rates than in Western Europe; the wage-rate differential between Eastern and Western Europe is actually much greater than that between Mexico and the United States. At the same time, Eastern Europe is positioned close to the heart of the Western European customer base.

On the other hand, France, Italy, and the United Kingdom have had the most rapid declines; the share of European production in these three countries declined from 54% in 1970 to 21% in 2012. These countries have had difficulty maintaining competitive cost structures in the face of greatly enhanced productivity in Germany and lower wage rates in Eastern Europe. Germany's share of European production in the 21st century is about the same as the combined share for East and West Germany in 1970.

Russia and Turkey are the principal producers of vehicles in Europe outside the EU. The auto industry in Russia is in part a legacy of the Soviet Union era when the communists emphasized investment in heavy industry. Soviet-era plants have been for the most part turned over to international carmakers, but most have been running well below capacity. European carmakers have constructed new plants. Turkey has also seen some new investment by European carmakers. European carmakers regard Russia and Turkey as potentially important centers for low-cost assembly, but they remain wary of investing in the countries because of an unstable investment climate.

Distribution of Production Within Asia

Worldwide production increased by 19 million vehicles during the first decade of the 21st century. Nearly all of the growth has been in Asia, where vehicle production increased from 18 million to 41 million during the period, whereas it declined from 18 million to 12 million in North America and remained unchanged at 20 million in Europe. As a result, the percentage of world production in Asia increased from 30% in 2000 to 53% in 2010. Asia had increased from 3% of world production in 1960 to 19% in 1970 and 31% in 1980, but the percentage did not change during the last two decades of the 20th century, before the rapid increase in the 21st century.

Within Asia, most vehicle production is distributed among a handful of countries (Figure 3.6). China accounts for 45% of Asian production, Japan for 20%, India and South Korea for 10% each, and Iran and Thailand for 5% each. Integration of vehicle production among countries within Asia has not occurred to the same extent as in Europe and North America. Long-standing political differences and military tensions have impeded cooperation in East Asia among Japan, South Korea, and China, as well as in South Asia between India and its neighbors. These issues have also induced consumers to avoid vehicles produced by adversarial countries.

Japan was responsible for most of Asia's car production increase during the 1960s and 1970s. Japan became the world's second leading producer during the 1960s, ahead of several European countries, and passed the United States to become the world leader during the 1970s. The United States and Japan maintained roughly comparable production levels through the end of the 20th century and into the first decade of the 21st century.

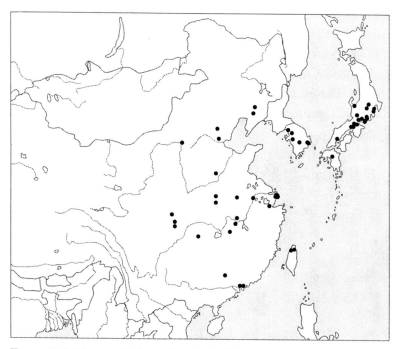

Figure 3.6 Motor vehicle production in East Asia

Source: Compiled by author from multiple sources.

Toyota dominates production in Japan, accounting for nearly half of the light vehicles assembled there. Most of the other half is divided roughly evenly among Honda, Mazda, Nissan, and Suzuki. Japan's carmakers have clustered most of their headquarters and production facilities in the Tokyo-Yokohama metropolitan area. The principal exception is Toyota, which has most of its facilities 250 kilometers to the west in the Nagoya area.

In India, vehicle production displays a pattern similar to that of Japan, with one company responsible for one-half of the market and several other companies at around 10% each. The leader in India is Maruti Suzuki India Limited, a company that began assembling vehicles in 1983. The company is jointly owned by Suzuki and the government of India. The other three leading carmakers in India are Hyundai, Tata Motors, and Mahindra & Mahindra.

When Maruti Suzuki began production, India's car market had been dominated first by Hindustan Motors and then by Premier Automobiles. These two companies assembled vehicles based on designs by the British firms Morris and Fiat, respectively. In both cases, models that were outdated when introduced were kept on the market for several decades. This left a wide opening for a newcomer to enter the market with an up-to-date model, and that proved to be Maruti.

Tata Motors, founded in 1945, is part of the Tata Group, one of the world's largest corporations. Tata specializes in commercial vehicles, though it has gained international attention by developing the Nano, considered the world's cheapest new car, selling at around $3,000 in 2012. Mahindra & Mahindra, founded in 1945, specialized in light trucks until 2007, when it started to assemble cars under a joint venture with Renault.

South Korea's auto industry is dominated by Hyundai Motor Group, which has 75% of the domestic market through its Hyundai and Kia brands. Hyundai operates what is considered the world's largest production facility at Ulsan, along the southeast coast.

China became the world's leading vehicle producer during the first decade of the 21st century. By 2010, China's output of more than 18 million vehicles exceeded the next two countries combined, the United States and Japan.

Vehicle production within China is not as clustered as in the other major producing regions. Around 25% of the country's production is in the Shanghai area, and the second-largest production center, with around 15% of the national total, is 1,500 kilometers to the north, around Changchun. The third-largest center, Beijing, is roughly midway between Shanghai and Changchun, and the fourth-largest center, around Chonqing, is 1,500 kilometers west of Shanghai.

Vehicles can be assembled in China only by Chinese-controlled companies. These companies can assemble vehicles that they develop and market, or they can assemble vehicles through joint ventures with foreign-owned carmakers. All 10 of the largest international carmakers, as well as several smaller ones, have joint ventures in China. Joint ventures involving GM and VW hold about 15% each of China's light vehicle market. Joint ventures with the other international carmakers together account for about 25% of the market. A dozen Chinese companies together have about 30% of the market, none with as much as 5%. The remaining 15% is scattered among numerous smaller firms.

The four leading Chinese carmakers are SAIC Motor, Dongfeng Motor, FAW Group, and Changan Automobile Group. These four companies together assemble around one-half of all vehicles in China, principally through joint ventures with international carmakers. SAIC (an acronym for Shanghai Automotive Industry Corporation), based in Shanghai, produces more than 20% of all light-vehicles in China primarily through joint ventures with GM, VW, and Fiat (through Iveco). Dongfeng, based in Wuhan, has joint ventures with Honda, Hyundai (through Kia), Nissan, and PSA Peugeot Citroën. FAW (an acronym for First Automobile Works), based in Changchun, has joint ventures with GM, Toyota, and VW. Changan, based in Chongqing, has joint ventures with Ford, PSA Peugeot Citroën, and Suzuki.

China's leading carmakers assembling and marketing primarily their own vehicles rather than joint ventures include Beiqi Foton Motor, Brilliance Jinbei Automobile, BYD Auto, Chery Automobile, Great Wall Motors, Jianghuai Automotive, and Zhejiang Geely Holding Group. These seven carmakers account for between 2% and 3% each, and a combined 20%, of China's light-vehicle production. Chery and Geely are best known outside of China, Chery because of efforts to export vehicles from

China to Europe and North America, and Geely because it owns the Volvo brand name.

Distribution of Production Within South America

Most of the world's vehicle production not clustered in the three principal regions described above is in South America. The region accounts for 5% of world production or all but 1% of the total not in Asia, Europe, and North America.

Within South America, Brazil is the dominant producer. Brazil is the seventh largest vehicle producing country and accounts for 4% of world production. Most of the remainder is in Argentina. Vehicle production in South America is controlled by the large international carmakers. High tariffs and domestic content requirements limit import of vehicles, so nearly all vehicles sold in the region are domestically assembled. Fiat, VW, and GM share more than 70% of Brazil's market. In Argentina, production is more evenly distributed as seven of the 10 leading international carmakers—PSA Peugeot Citroën, GM, VW, Renault, Toyota, Ford, and Fiat— produce between 10% and 17% of the vehicles.

Labor Relations in the Auto Industry

Most of the world's assembly plant workers belong to a trade union. The principal exception is North America, where fewer than half of assembly plant workers are union members. Relatively few workers in parts supplier plants belong to a union.

Early cars were put together by skilled craftsmen. Pattern makers, molders, core makers, and forge operators fashioned unique parts for each individual car. Machinists finished rough castings into an engine and transmission. Woodworkers, painters, and upholsterers fashioned the body. Mechanics fitted the handmade parts into a finished car at a stationary work station.

Because of their specialized knowledge and skills, early craft workers were able to set the pace and accuracy of production. They used this power to force higher wages, reduced working hours, and beneficial job roles. Skilled craft production was replaced with specialized, repetitive, and automatic work, requiring little thought, judgment, or skill.

Motor vehicle production was transformed during the early 20th century from skilled to unskilled work. Most critical in deskilling the workforce was the introduction of the moving assembly line in 1914 by the Ford Motor Co. Each worker was positioned at a particular spot along the moving line and assigned a specific task in the assembly of the vehicle to perform repeatedly. The organization of auto factory work using minimally skilled labor became known as Taylorism, after Frederick W. Taylor, known as the father of scientific management. Taylor's influential book published in 1911, *The Principles of Scientific Management*, recommended breaking down factory jobs, based on careful time and motion studies, into simple repetitive tasks capable of being performed by minimally skilled laborers.

With deskilling of the production process, workers lost control of the workplace. In reaction, workers in the motor vehicle industry were among the first to organize unions around an industrial sector. Nineteenth century unions were organized around crafts such as painting and metal finishing, a legacy of medieval craft guilds and apprenticeships. With the rise of mass production in the 20th century, most notably in the auto industry, unions were organized to represent workers in industrial sectors such as steel and mining, regardless of the specific task they performed in the factory.

Labor Relations in the North American Auto Industry

The mind-numbing and physically debilitating work along Ford's moving assembly line resulted in an extremely high turnover rate. Ford retained workers by paying them $5 a day in 1914, more than twice the average factory wage rate at the time. However, the Great Depression that followed the 1929 stock market crash brought widespread layoffs, and those still employed suffered from harsher working conditions and lower wages. In reaction, efforts to unionize auto workers gained momentum, and New Deal legislation and policies provided legal protection for organizing. In the U.S. auto industry, organizing efforts culminated in 1937 into GM's recognition of the United Auto Workers (UAW) union following a sit-down strike at several GM parts plants. Chrysler quickly followed in recognizing the union. After several years of violent confrontations, Ford workers voted to join the UAW in 1941.

During the second half of the 20th century, the UAW and U.S. carmakers negotiations followed a pattern. As three-year contracts were about to expire, the UAW would select one company as the bargaining target. The target company was threatened with a strike if negotiations failed, whereas production would continue at the other carmakers. Once agreement was reached with the targeted company, the other carmakers would be offered the same contract. Pattern bargaining resulted in ever more favorable contracts. Prosperous carmakers were willing to share profits to buy labor peace. Workers were offered and accepted a deal: work hard at mindless, thankless jobs for 30 years in exchange for high wages, health care for the entire family, and generous pensions. U.S. and Canadian auto workers ranked among the world's highest paid and best protected factory workers. Canadian auto workers split off from the UAW to form a separate Canadian Auto Workers Union in 1985.

The success of the Japanese at producing and selling vehicles in North America ended the half-century pattern of bargaining between the UAW and U.S. carmakers. No Japanese-owned assembly plants in North America were unionized. By the 21st century, North American assembly plants were divided into a unionized half owned by the Detroit Three carmakers and a nonunionized half owned by Asian and German carmakers. Uncompetitive labor contracts were one of the factors leading to the bankruptcy of Chrysler and GM in 2009.

Labor Relations in Europe's Auto Industries

European auto workers are nearly all unionized, and they are protected by relatively strong laws compared to other carmaking regions. Wages are higher in Western Europe than in other regions, though wages lag in formerly Communist Eastern Europe. Because labor laws require that they be consulted extensively, auto unions in Europe can successfully resist management attempts to lay off workers or close plants. Layoffs and closures do not eliminate requirements to pay the workers, so management is likely to keep open a plant with limited production.

In Germany, a large nationwide union IG Metall (Industrial Union of Metalworkers) represents much of the automotive workers as well as those in other manufacturing industries. German labor law grants union representatives half the seats on companies' supervisory boards. Every factory has a council where management and employees collaborate on working conditions.

In France as a whole, only 5% of private sector workers are members of unions, but unions represent most auto workers. To be recognized as a representative union in France, at least 10% of the workforce in an industrial sector must vote to support that particular union. The five largest confederations of unions in France are—in order of number of members—CGT (General Confederation of Labor), CFDT (French Democratic Confederation of Labor), CFTC (French Confederation of Christian Workers), CGT-FO (General Confederation of Labor—Workers' Force), and CFE-CGC (French Confederation of Management—General Confederation of Executives). All five represent auto workers. Consequently, management must negotiate with multiple unions of varying degrees of militancy and positions on specific issues.

In Italy, national federations of unions are affiliated with the various political parties, including Christian Democrat-affiliated Italian Confederation of Trade Unions (CISL), Communist-affiliated Italian General Confederation of Labor (CGIL), and Socialist-affiliated Italian Labor Union (UIL). Fiat workers are represented by a collection of unions of metalworkers affiliated with the various political groups, including Christian Democratic (FIM-CISL), Communist (FIOM), and Socialist (UILM) as well as Fascist (UGL) and politically unaffiliated (FISMIC).

Labor Relations in Asia's Auto Industries

Japan does not have a tradition of independent labor unions. Prior to World War II, individual companies had factory councils organized by management. After the war, the victorious Allies imposed democratic legislation, giving Japanese workers the right to organize independent trade unions as bargaining agents. Separate unions were set up at the various carmakers, replacing the factory councils. The company-specific unions have joined together in a confederation Jidosha Soren (Confederation of Japan Automobile Workers' Unions).

The Japanese auto industry has been in the forefront in replacing long-standing so-called Fordist or mass production practices with flexible or lean production. Japanese companies were inspired to adopt flexible production by W. Edwards Deming (1900–1993). Deming introduced Japanese engineers and managers to concepts of quality. He showed that higher quality would have a positive impact on net income through improved productivity and increased sales. In fact, as the first carmakers to adopt flexible production, Japanese companies were able to increase sales internationally, especially during the late 20th century, by selling vehicles that consumers and independent testing organizations found to have higher quality than vehicles produced by U.S.- and Europe-based companies.

Flexible production has reduced the ability of trade unions to negotiate workplace rules such as allocating jobs by seniority and requiring 10-minute breaks every hour. Instead of allocating to each individual worker a specific repetitive task, under flexible production a team of workers is assigned a set of tasks. The team is given responsibility for organizing itself in order to perform the collection of tasks. One of the team members is appointed team leader and performs coordination tasks. Productivity has increased, because teams are constantly working on a variety of tasks. Under mass production, a worker might stand idle waiting for someone down the line to catch up, and jobs were allocated according to seniority rather than skill.

China has a single official union, the government-controlled All-China Federation of Trade Unions (ACFTU). The union has branches in various regions and industrial sectors. European and American unions do not consider ACFTU to be independent. Union leaders are appointed by the Communist Party rather than elected by workers. Workers may not choose to organize and join another union if they prefer. The union does not negotiate collective bargaining agreements. The ACFTU operates in most of China's assembly plants. ACFTU officials in the assembly plants act as consultants to management on concerns of wages and working conditions. The ACFTU is not represented in most of the supplier plants.

CHAPTER 4

Organization of the Motor Vehicle Industry: Sales

This chapter focuses on the organization of the sale of the world's motor vehicles. Included in this chapter are discussions of the distribution of vehicles around the world and the structures for their distribution.

As fragile, bulky, fabricated products, motor vehicles are produced near where they are sold. The cardinal rule among carmakers is to build vehicles near where they are to be sold. Thus, more than 90% of sales—as production—is clustered in Asia, Europe, and North America, and Latin America accounts for most of the remainder. Africa, with 15% of the world's population, accounts for only 2% of the world's vehicle sales. Nonetheless, the global distribution of motor vehicle sales does not exactly match the distribution of production. Some regions produce more cars than are sold, whereas other regions have higher sales than production.

Registration and Ownership of Vehicles

Roughly 3 billion motor vehicles have been built worldwide through the century-plus of motor vehicle production. Slightly more than 1 billion of these vehicles are currently registered. Asia, Europe, and North America each has around 300 million vehicles, leaving around 100 million in Africa and Latin America. The United States has the largest number of vehicles, around 240 million. Thus, the United States, with 4% of the world's population, has 24% of the world's vehicles. China and Japan follow the United States in the number of vehicles, with 78 million and 74 million, respectively.

The number of motor vehicles in the world is approximately 170 per 1,000 persons. The developed regions of Europe and North America have a combined ratio of 630 vehicles per 1,000 persons compared to a ratio of 80 vehicles per 1,000 persons overall in the developing regions,

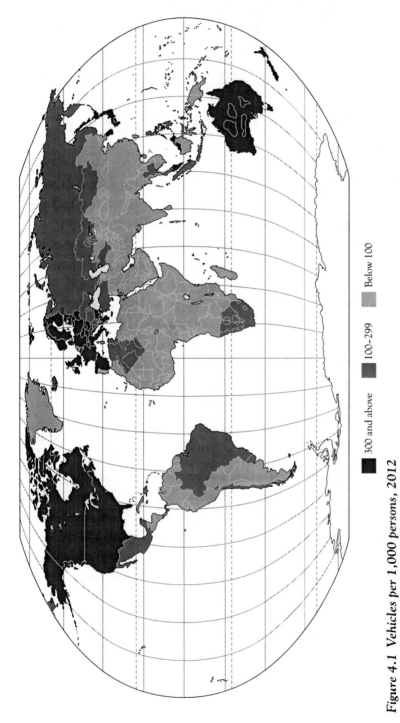

Figure 4.1 Vehicles per 1,000 persons, 2012

Source: World Bank at http://data.worldbank.org/indicator/IS.VEH.NVEH.P3/countries?display=default

300 and above   100–299   Below 100

Africa, Asia, and Latin America. Otherwise stated, there is 1 vehicle for every 6 persons in the world as a whole, 1 for every 1.6 persons in the developed regions and 1 for every 12.5 persons in the developing regions (Figure 4.1).

Among the world's most populous countries, the United States has by far the most vehicles per capita, approximately 800 per 1,000 persons, or 1 vehicle per 1.3 persons. Among the 10 most populous countries, Japan ranks second in vehicles per capita, with 600 vehicles per 1,000 persons, or 1 vehicle per 1.7 persons. Unique among populous countries, the number of vehicles in the United States (approximately 250 million) far exceeds the number of licensed drivers (approximately 200 million). Japan has just over 1 vehicle per licensed driver.

At the other extreme, vehicle ownership rates are very low in the most populous countries of Asia. The number of vehicles per 1,000 persons is 85 in China, 60 in Indonesia, 18 in India and Pakistan, and 3 in Bangladesh. That's 1 vehicle per 12 persons in China, per 17 persons in Indonesia, per 56 persons in India and Pakistan, and per 333 persons in Bangladesh. Forecasts of rapid future growth in world motor vehicle registrations derive primarily from projections of increased ownership rates in these very populous countries of Asia. An increase of 1 per 1,000 in the vehicle ownership rate in each of these five Asian countries would add 3 million vehicles to the total world registration.

Motor vehicles must be registered with a government agency in order to be legally driven. The authority responsible for registering vehicles is a state or provincial government agency in North America and a national government agency in most other countries. As part of the registration process, license plates issued by the authority must be displayed on the vehicle. France issued the first license plates in 1893, and Germany followed three years later. U.S. states began to issue them in 1903. In some countries, the plates remain the same throughout the vehicle's life, passing from one owner to the next, whereas other jurisdictions require that the plates be changed when the vehicle is sold. In North America, the plates are updated annually, either with a sticker or an entirely new set of plates.

Sales Volume and Trade of Vehicles

For most consumers, a motor vehicle is their second most expensive purchase after a house. In developed countries, the median cost of a new vehicle amounts to a little less than the median annual household income. In developing countries, the cost is five times more than income.

Motor Vehicle Sales

Worldwide sales of new motor vehicles totaled 82 million in 2012. Most vehicles pass through more than one owner. In the United States, 40 million used vehicles were sold in 2011, three times more than the number of new vehicles. Applying the same 3:1 ratio worldwide would produce a global estimate of 250 million used vehicle sales.

Approximately 38 million new vehicles were sold in Asia (including Oceania) in 2012, 19 million in Europe (including Russia), 18 million in North America (including Mexico), 6 million in Central and South America, and 3 million in Africa (Table 4.1). China is by far the world's largest market for vehicles. Sales totaled 19 million in China in 2012, 24% of overall world sales. The United States is second in the world with 15 million sales in 2012, that is 18% of the world total, followed by Japan with 5 million sales, that is 7% of the world total. Countries with between 2 million and 4 million annual sales include Brazil, France, Germany, India, Russia, and the United Kingdom.

Worldwide figures for vehicle sales do not match the distribution of production. In 2012, Asia produced 44 million new vehicles and bought 38 million, Europe produced 20 million and bought 19 million, North America produced 16 million and bought 18 million, Central and South America produced 4 million and bought 6 million, and Africa produced 1 million and bought 3 million. Thus, on balance, more vehicles are assembled than sold in Asia and Europe, and fewer are assembled than sold elsewhere in the world.

As with production, the distribution of motor vehicle sales has changed sharply in the past quarter-century. In 1990, worldwide sales of new motor vehicles totaled 49 million. Approximately 12 million vehicles were sold in Asia (including Oceania) in 1990, 19 million in Europe (including Russia), 16 million in North America (including Mexico), 1 million

Table 4.1 Sales by country, 2012

Asia	
China	19.3
Japan	5.4
India	3.6
South Korea	1.5
Thailand	1.4
Australia	1.1
Other Asia	5.7
Europe	
Germany	3.4
Russia	3.1
France	2.3
United Kingdom	2.3
Italy	1.5
Other Europe	6.1
North America	
United States	14.8
Canada	1.7
Other North America	0.9
Other regions	
Brazil	3.8
Other countries	5.2
Total	81.7

Note: Figures are in million vehicles.

Source: International Organization of Motor Vehicle Manufacturers (http://www.oica.net/).

in Central and South America, and 1 million in Africa (Figure 4.2). Thus, during the past quarter-century, vehicle sales have stagnated in Europe and in North America, but they have increased from 12 to 38 million vehicles in Asia, from 1 to 6 million in Central and South America, and from 1 to 3 million in Africa.

Annual sales of new vehicles reached historically high levels in North America and Europe in 2005 and 2007, respectively. In Europe, sales peaked in 2007 at 23 million and declined in the following years by around one-fifth. The lingering effect of the severe recession that began in 2008 has continued to depress new vehicle sales in Europe. The declines have been especially severe in Southern European countries, including Greece, Italy, Portugal, and Spain, where the recession was especially severe and long-lasting. Sales declined more sharply in North America than in Europe during the severe 2008–2009 recession by 40% in North

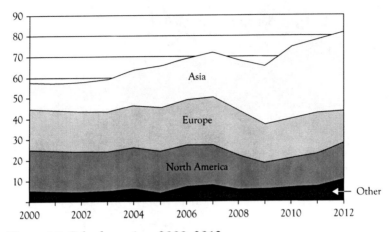

Figure 4.2 Sales by region, 2000–2012

Source: Compiled by author from multiple issues of *Automotive News*.

America compared with 20% in Europe. But sales have recovered to near the pre recession level in North America, whereas sales have continued to stagnate in Europe.

New vehicle sales in China exceeded 5 million for the first time in 2005, 10 million for the first time in 2009, and 20 million anticipated in 2013. China passed Germany as the third-leading new vehicle market in 2004, Japan as the second-leading market in 2006, and the United States as the leading market in 2009. The share of the world's vehicles sold in China increased from 10% in 2005 to 24% in 2010. One-third of the worldwide growth in vehicle sales during the next decade is expected to come from China.[1]

International Trade in Motor Vehicles

On a global scale, net trade of vehicles among regions is relatively modest. The numbers of vehicles produced and sold are roughly equal within Europe. More vehicles are produced in Asia than are sold in that region, whereas more vehicles are sold than produced in the rest of the world (North America, Latin America, and Africa). The net movement of vehicles among these regions amounts to less than 10% of total world production and sales. On balance, approximately 7 million vehicles of the 80 million produced and sold worldwide are exported from Asia into North America, Latin America, and Africa (Table 4.2).[2]

Table 4.2 Distribution of production and sales by world region, 2012

Region	Production (%)	Sales (%)
Asia (including Oceania)	52	44
Europe (including Russia)	24	24
North America	19	21
Latin America	5	8
Africa	1	4

Source: Compiled by author from International Organization of Motor Vehicle Manufacturers (http://www.oica.net/).

The relatively modest global net trade figure masks larger flows of vehicles among regions, as well as even more substantial movement of vehicles among countries within regions. At the interregional scale, approximately 15 million of the 80 million vehicles sold in 2012 were produced outside of the region of the sale. From Asia, roughly 3 million vehicles were exported to North America, 3 million to Europe, and 1 million each to Latin America and Africa. Approximately 2 million vehicles were shipped from Europe to North America and 1 million from North America to Europe. Approximately 2 million each were exported from North America to Latin America and from Europe to Africa (Figure 4.3).

The import of vehicles from other regions is impeded by barriers that can raise the price of imported vehicles to uncompetitive levels. Tariffs contribute to higher prices in some countries, including the United States, but the principal cause of higher prices for vehicles imported from other regions is homologation. Homologation is government certification that a particular vehicle matches specified criteria to which all vehicles sold in that country must conform. The challenge for carmakers is that criteria vary among countries and regions. The variations could be relatively minor and inexpensive to address, such as the shape of the license plate holder. However, some variations are extremely costly for carmakers, such as the type of glass that can be used for the windshield.

Restrictions and tariffs in the movement of vehicles between the United States and Canada were eliminated during the 1960s. The North American Free Trade Agreement (NAFTA), implemented during the 1990s, eliminated barriers to the trade of vehicles among the United States, Canada, and Mexico.

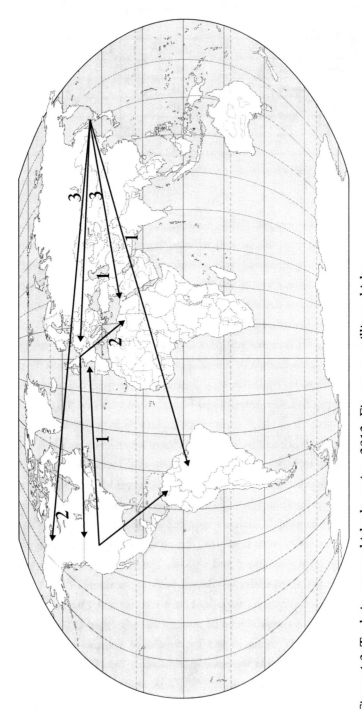

Figure 4.3 Trade in motor vehicles by region, 2012. Figures are million vehicles

Source: Compiled by author from multiple government trade data sources.

Prior to the 1960s, Canada's auto industry was organized separately from that of the United States, and high tariffs limited imports into Canada. A Canadian government commission in the early 1960s concluded that the country's auto plants, which were all owned by U.S. companies, were unprofitable and at risk of closure. Because of the small size of the domestic market, Canadian plants had to produce a wide variety of vehicles in unprofitable and inefficient small batches. As a result, Canada signed an agreement with the United States to eliminate tariffs on vehicles and parts. Of more significance to Canada, U.S.-owned carmakers signed letters of understanding agreeing to guarantee a minimum level of production in Canada.

Mexico attempted to support its auto industry during the 1970s and 1980s through a series of decrees that alternated between raising and lowering requirements for the minimum percentage of local content in vehicles sold in Mexico and for the maximum percentage of vehicles that could be imported and exported duty-free. Foreign-owned carmakers increased investment in Mexico primarily in the early 1980s and again in the early 1990s.

With implementation of NAFTA in the 1990s, Mexico's vehicle market was fully integrated with those of the United States and Canada. In 2012, 1 million vehicles were sold in Mexico, approximately evenly divided among imported and domestic. Production in Mexico was 2.7 million vehicles in 2012. With around 0.5 million sold domestically, 2.2 million (i.e., 81% of production) were exported primarily to the United States.

Approximately 4 million of the 17 million vehicles sold in North America in 2012 were imported, including approximately 2.5 million from Asia and 1.5 million from Europe. Nearly all imported vehicles were passenger cars rather than light trucks. The United States imposes a tariff of 2.5% on cars and 25% on pickup trucks and vans imported from countries other than Canada and Mexico. The extremely high tariff on trucks is a legacy of the so-called chicken tax. In 1962, several European countries, including France and Germany, raised tariffs on imported chickens, effectively eliminating access to European markets for the U.S. poultry industry. A year later, the United States retaliated by setting a high tariff on a collection of products imported into the United States that had a value equivalent to U.S. chicken exports to Europe at the time, and that turned out to include pickup trucks. When the chicken tax was imposed, the primary target was German-made VW vehicles, but as Asian carmakers became the leading exporters to the United States, they were most affected.

Approximately 3 million vehicles are exported from North America, including around 2 million from the United States and 1 million from Mexico. Exports are destined primarily for Europe and Latin America. Mexico is playing an increasingly important role as a center for exporting motor vehicles. In 2012, 83% of vehicles assembled in Mexico were exported (including those sent to the United States), the highest percentage for any country and the fourth highest in volume behind Germany, Japan, and South Korea. Carmakers are attracted to Mexico as a location for assembly plants, primarily because Mexico has free trade agreements with 44 government entities, including the European Union, as of 2012.

Within Europe, a large percentage of vehicles produced in one country are sold in other European countries, but relatively few vehicles are imported from or exported to other regions of the world. Of the 19 million vehicles sold in Europe, 3 million are imported, nearly all from Japan and Korea. Of the 20 million produced in Europe, 4 million are exported, around 1 million to North America and 3 million to Asia.

Barriers to the movement of vehicles from one country to another within the European Union were eliminated. However, the European Union has a 10% tariff on vehicles imported from other regions, including the United States.

Unlike the other two major vehicle-producing regions, a large percentage of vehicles produced in Asia are exported to other regions, but relatively few move from one country to another within the region. Around 5 million vehicles, two-thirds of the country's production, were exported from Japan. Shipments from Japan included 2 million to North America, 1 million each to Europe and other Asia-Pacific countries, and 0.5 million each to Latin America and to Africa. South Korea is also one of the world's leading exporters; 3 million of the country's 5 million total vehicle production is exported. South Korea's distribution of shipments among regions was close to the pattern for Japan. By contrast, only around 1 million of the 18 million vehicles produced in China in 2012 were exported, nearly all to Asia.

China imposes a 25% tariff on the import of vehicles. Japan has no tariffs on importing vehicles. Instead, it has especially challenging homologation rules that result in doubling the price of vehicles, thereby effectively curtailing imports of all but a few luxury models.

Vehicle Classification

Vehicles are sold in a wide variety of sizes, styles, and prices. Gone are the days when one model, Ford's Model T, accounted for half of the world's sales. The French magazine *Auto Moto* identified 100 models sold in 2013 by the world's 10 best-selling companies, and another 100 by others. Excluded are many more companies that sell only a handful of vehicles.

Market Segmentation

The terminology for identifying vehicles and classifying them into segments is not standardized by government agencies, carmakers, or trade organizations. The most popular vehicles are identified informally by carmakers and trade publications with the letters A through F. These distinguish vehicles by a combination of size and price.

- A is a minicar such as Fiat 500.
- B is a subcompact car in North America and a small car in Europe such as Ford Fiesta.
- C is a compact in North America and a lower medium or small family car in Europe such as Ford Focus.
- D is a mid-sized car in North America and an upper medium or a large family car in Europe such as Honda Accord.
- E is a compact luxury car in North America and an entry premium car in Europe such as BMW 3 series.
- F is a mid-sized luxury car in North America and a medium premium car in Europe such as BMW 5 series.

The most popular sizes in Europe are B and C, each accounting for roughly one-fourth of all sales. In Japan, the C segment has around 40% of all sales. In North America, the two most popular sizes, C and D, account for only around one-sixth of sales each. Light trucks account for nearly half of sales in North America, compared to only around 10% in the rest of the world.

Carmakers often blur distinctions among the six letters by deliberately creating models with dimensions that fall between two letters. They also sell vehicles that are more sporty or rugged than the archetypal models of a particular letter classification. Vehicles are also sold that are distinctive to one region of the world.

Recognizing that carmakers have created numerous segments that do not fall neatly into one of the six letter sizes, *Automotive News* identifies 26 segments of vehicles sold in North America and 22 in Europe. Thirteen of the segments in North America are considered cars, and 13 are considered light trucks. In Europe, 11 each of the *Automotive News* segments are cars and light trucks. In North America, around one-half of the sales are accounted for by 4 of the 26 segments: compact (C class such as Ford Focus), mid-sized (D class such as Ford Fusion), full-sized pickup (such as Ford F series), and crossover utility vehicle (such as Ford Escape). In Europe, around one-half of the sales are accounted for by just two of the 22 segments, which correspond to the international C and D class designations. Half of the segments in Europe and North America hold less than 1% of the respective region's market.

Government regulations can influence classification. In Japan, for example, most vehicles are classified as 1 through 5 based on the prefix of the license plate. A "1" is a large truck, a "2" is a bus, a "3" is a large car, a "4" is a small truck, and a "5" is a small car. Each of the 5 segments pays a different tax. In the United States, carmakers designate vehicles as trucks or cars because the two classifications have separate fuel efficiency standards.

Corporate Branding

Each company typically markets its vehicles by make (or brand), model (or nameplate), and trim. For example, a Honda Civic DX identifies Honda as the make, Civic as the model, and DX as the trim. "Honda" doubles as the corporate name as well as the make. Honda, the carmaker, also sells vehicles with the Acura brand. Similarly, a Ford Focus S identifies Ford as the make, Focus as the model, and S as the trim. The Ford Motor Company also sells vehicles with the Lincoln brand. Most major carmakers use their corporate name for their best-selling brand. The leading exception is GM, which rarely doubles its corporate name as a brand.

Carmakers also classify vehicles by platform. A platform is the chassis and other underpinnings of the vehicle upon which a variety of bodies and powertrains can be attached. Vehicles in several segments can share a single platform. For example, the Ford Focus car and Ford C-Max truck are based on the same platform, known inside the Ford Motor Company as C1. Designing a variety of vehicles from a single platform enables carmakers to save considerable development costs. At the same time, the shared components are largely invisible to consumers, so vehicles on a single platform appear and perform differently for consumers.

Ford Motor Co. accounted for half of the vehicles sold in the United States and in the world during the 1910s with only one make, one model, and one platform—the Ford Model T. Henry Ford envisioned the motor vehicle as something useful rather than stylish. He famously sold the Model T in only black for most of its 18 years of production, because black took less time to dry than other paint.

General Motors passed Ford in sales during the 1920s in part by offering a variety of makes and models. Alfred P. Sloan, GM's long-time President and Chairman of the Board, called GM's marketing strategy "a car for every purse and purpose."[3] For 75 years, GM prospered by selling five makes—Chevrolet, Pontiac, Oldsmobile, Buick, and Cadillac—listed here in order from least to most expensive. Chevrolet was marketed as affordable, Pontiac as stylish, Oldsmobile as well-engineered, Buick as refined, and Cadillac as elite. Each of the five makes offered a variety of distinctively named models—for example, Chevrolet in 1955 had the 150 series, 210 series, and Bel Air models—but the differences among these so-called models were what would now be considered variations in trim.

Beginning around 1960, North American carmakers began to sell models within makes in a variety of platforms as well as price points. Four principal platforms emerged, known at the time as subcompact, compact, mid-sized (or intermediate), and full-sized (or large). In 1970, for example, the Chevrolet make included the subcompact Vega, the compact Nova, the intermediate Chevelle, and the full-sized "regular" Chevrolet. Several specialty and limited production vehicles were also marketed. In the wake of gas shortages and price rises in the 1970s, U.S. carmakers reduced the dimensions of the four main types of vehicles. The rising popularity of substituting trucks for passenger cars added to the variety of models in the late 20th century.

Top Vehicles by Market

The market share held by the leading companies varies among the major markets around the world as do their individual makes or brands and their nameplates or models.[4]

- These companies had at least 5% of the national or regional market in 2013:
  - In the United States, GM had 18%, Ford 16%, Toyota 14%, Chrysler 12%, Honda 10%, Hyundai 8%, and Nissan 8% (Figure 4.4).
  - In Europe, VW had 26%; Renault (including Nissan) 12%; PSA Peugeot Citroën 11%; GM 8%; Ford 7%; and BMW, Daimler-Benz, Fiat, and Hyundai 6% each (Figure 4.5).
  - In Japan, Toyota had 43% and Honda, Nissan, and Suzuki had 13% each (Figure 4.6).
  - In China, the corporate level needs to be counted in two ways because of the preponderance of joint ventures between international and domestically owned carmakers. Among Chinese-owned companies, Shanghai Automotive

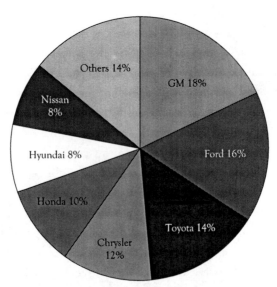

Figure 4.4 Market share by company in the United States, 2013

Source: Compiled by author from *Automotive News*.

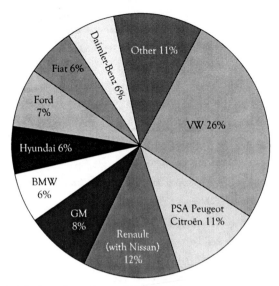

Figure 4.5 Market share by company in Europe, 2013

Source: Compiled by author from *Automotive News*.

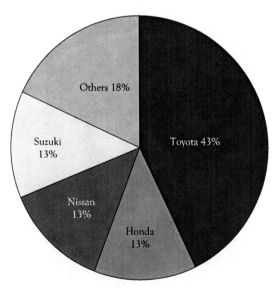

Figure 4.6 Market share by company in Japan, 2013

Source: Compiled by author from Japan Auto Manufacturers Association.

had 23% of the market, Dongfeng 14%, FAW 12%, Changan 10%, and Beijing Automotive 8%. Among international carmakers, VW's joint ventures with several of the above-listed Chinese companies amounted to 14% of the market and joint ventures from the above list involving GM and Hyundai 7% each (Figure 4.7).

- These makes or brands had at least 5% of the market in 2013:
  - In the United States, Ford had 15%, GM's Chevrolet 13%, Toyota 12%, Honda 9%, Nissan 7%, and Hyundai 5%.
  - In Europe, VW had 13%; Ford and GM's Opel 7% each; Peugeot, Renault, and VW's Audi 6% each; and BMW, Fiat, Mercedes-Benz, and Peugeot's Citroen 5% each.
  - In Japan, Toyota had 29% and Daihatsu, Honda, Nissan, and Suzuki had 13% each.
  - In China, only three brands had at least 5% of the market: VW with 11%, Wuling with 7%, and Hyundai with 5%.
- These models or nameplates had at least 2% of the market in 2013:
  - In the United States, Ford F-150 pickup truck had 5% and GM's Chevrolet Silverado pickup truck and Toyota Camry

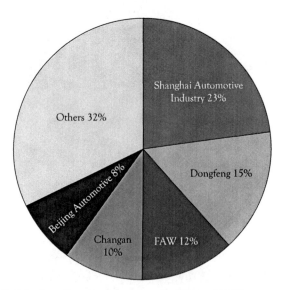

Figure 4.7 Market share by company in China, 2013

Source: Compiled by author from *Automotive News*.

D-class car 3% each. With 2% each were the D-class Ford
Fusion, Honda Accord, Nissan Altima, and Toyota Prius; the
C-class Ford Focus, GM's Chevrolet Cruze, Honda Civic,
Hyundai Elantra, and Toyota Corolla; the Ford Escape,
GM's Chevrolet Equinox, and Honda CR-V crossover utility
vehicles; and Chrysler's Ram pickup truck.

○ In Europe, the C-class VW Golf and the B-class Ford Fiesta
each had 3% of the market. With 2% each were the A-class
Renault Clio, Fiat Punto, and Opel Corsa; the B-class VW
Polo, Peugeot 207, and Fiat Panda; and the C-class Ford
Focus and Renault Megane.

○ In Japan, the D-class Toyota Prius and C-class Toyota
Aqua (called the Prius C in the United States) had 5% of
the market each. The B-class Honda Fit and Nissan Note
(called the Versa in the United States) had 3% each. The
Nissan Serena minivan, the F-class Toyota Crown, and the
B-class Toyota Vitz had 2% each.

○ In China, the only models to have at least 2% of the
market in 2012 were four small trucks. Wuling Sunshine
had 3% and Foton Forland and Wuling Hongguang and
Rongguang/Xingwang had 2% each.

Dealership Networks

Dealerships are independent businesses that purchase vehicles from the
factory at wholesale prices and sell them to customers at retail prices. Carmakers set a manufacturer's suggested retail price (MSRP), but customers
rarely pay this amount. As with housing, most vehicles are sold at prices
negotiated between buyers and sellers. The profit margin for a dealer on
the sale of new vehicles is thin, in the magnitude of 1%–3%. However,
carmakers often reduce the wholesale price of vehicles sold to dealers,
especially for slow-selling models.

Each dealer has an exclusive franchise to sell a carmaker's vehicles
within a specified territory. Within that territory, no other dealer is
allowed to have a showroom that displays or sells the same carmaker's
vehicles. In exchange for the exclusive franchise, the dealer agrees to
purchase a predetermined number of vehicles, maintain an agreed-upon

inventory of replacement parts, and repair vehicles at agreed-upon prices using factory-authorized parts. The dealer also agrees to display signs, arrange the showroom, and run advertising consistent with the carmaker's marketing strategy. The sales staff are paid primarily, if not exclusively, on commission.

The mean gross sales in 2012 for a franchised dealership in the United States were $38.4 million. The sale of new vehicles had revenues of $21.6 million, or 56% of total sales, at the average dealership. The average dealership also generated revenues of $12.2 million from the sale of used vehicles and $4.6 million from performing service and selling parts. The pretax profit for the average U.S. dealership in 2012 was $843,697, only 2.2% of sales. Sales of used vehicles, service, and parts accounted for disproportionately large shares of the profits.[5]

Most vehicles are sold in North America on credit. Most often, the dealer handles the financing arrangements as part of the transaction although some customers obtain loans directly from commercial banks or other financial institutions. Availability of credit was one of the most important elements in the rapid growth of sales in the United States during the first decades of the 20th century. To meet the growing demand for credit, GM established the General Motors Acceptance Corporation (GMAC) in 1919. GMAC extended credit to dealers to carry inventories and to consumers to cover new vehicle purchases. Other carmakers subsequently established in-house financing agencies. Dealers typically check with both commercial banks and in-house agencies to secure the most favorable rate for their customers.

Early cars were sold alongside bicycles, in department stores, hardware stores, and other general purpose retailers. This arrangement was unsatisfactory for both consumers and manufacturers: retailers needed more expertise, because early vehicles were unreliable, difficult to operate, and most of all simply unfamiliar to nearly all buyers. After a period of experimentation in the first two decades of the 20th century, vehicles have been sold in the United States almost exclusively through franchised dealers.

A dealership has three ways to generate income: sell new vehicles, sell used vehicles, and perform service. The sale of new vehicles accounts for 55%–60% of revenues, the sale of used vehicles 25%–30%, and the provision of service 10%–15%. Profits are distributed differently: 30% from new vehicle sales, 25% from used sales, and 45% from service.[6]

Approximately 17,000 dealers are in operation in the United States, holding 31,000 franchises. The large difference between the number of dealers and the number of franchises is because dealers are allowed to hold franchises for more than one nameplate used by a particular company. For example, Chrysler has 9,000 franchises but only 2,300 dealers, because all but a handful of them sell all four of the company's nameplates (Chrysler, Dodge, Jeep, and Ram). Overall, approximately 10,000 dealers sell Detroit three nameplates and 7,000 sell international nameplates.

Dealerships have traditionally been small businesses. Nearly all of the 47,000 dealerships in 1950 were owned by individuals who held one franchise to sell one brand of vehicle in their hometowns. The 17,760 dealerships in the United States in 2013 were owned by approximately 7,000 companies. The most typical arrangement is for a company to operate two or three dealerships with one selling Detroit Three nameplates and another selling those of an international carmaker.

The mean number of vehicles sold per dealer in the United States in 2012 was approximately 900. This compares with approximately 100 vehicles per dealer in 1950 and 300 in 1980. The rapid increase is a reflection in part of the two-thirds decline in the number of dealerships, but the larger share stems from increasing sales. The largest dealership company in the United States, AutoNation, owned 221 dealerships in 2012 and sold 267,810 vehicles. Three other companies—Penske Automotive Group, Sonic Automotive, and Group 1 Automotive—each held at least 100 dealerships and sold more than 100,000 vehicles. The 100 largest dealers together accounted for around 2.4 million sales, or 16% of the national total in 2012.

Economies of scale have pushed the consolidation of dealerships. Competition from the increased number of carmakers has driven down net profit per vehicle. The service department—the profit center for most dealerships—requires expensive equipment to diagnose and repair problems, which are increasingly electronic rather than mechanical in modern vehicles. Dealerships get more favorable terms from carmakers if they sell at higher volumes.

At the same time, franchise laws in most U.S. states protect dealers from national consolidation. A dealer holding a franchise in one market may not solicit customers in other markets. A customer who chooses to travel to another market to buy a vehicle must pay the taxes applicable to purchasing a vehicle in the hometown. As a result, unlike most other retail sectors such as electronics and clothing, national dealership brands have not been created.

The density of dealerships has been much higher in Europe than in the United States. In 2000, for example, Europe had more than 100,000 franchises, compared to 30,000 in the United States. Franchises in Europe have been divided roughly evenly between dealers and sub-dealers. The franchised dealers have played a role as wholesalers for sub-dealers located in small towns and rural areas. Subdealerships were especially common in France and Italy as outlets for the national brands (Citroën, Peugeot, and Renault in France, and Fiat in Italy).

Consolidation of dealerships has been occurring at a rapid rate in Europe in the 21st century. European Commission regulations adopted in 2002 and implemented in 2005 enabled dealers to hold franchises for more than one brand, as in the United States. In the wake of the new regulations, one-fifth of the dealerships in Europe closed between 2002 and 2005. As national brands such as Fiat and Renault lost their dominant market positions in their home countries, many of their subdealers closed. The lingering effects of the severe recession of 2008–2009 have induced more closures. In Italy, for example, the number of dealerships declined by 31% between 2008 and 2013.

Ford, the innovator in so many aspects of the industry, tried to sell vehicles directly to consumers in company owned stores in the early 20th century. The arrangement proved impractical. Sales people on the Ford payroll were found by the company to have less incentive than independent dealers to sell more cars and watch expenses. Ford's biggest challenge, though, was that the rapid growth in demand for vehicles outpaced the ability of the company to open and staff stores.

Company-owned stores persist in countries other than the United States. In Europe, 2%–3% of dealerships are company-owned. In Germany, Daimler-Benz owns 98 dealerships that employ 16,000 people and accounts for half of the company's sales in its home country. BMW has

43 company-owned dealerships that account for one-quarter of its sales in Germany. Company-owned stores are not profitable in Germany, and the carmakers are looking to sell some of them to independent dealers.

In Japan, the carmakers exercise more control over sales. Most cars in Japan were traditionally sold door-to-door by sales representatives employed by the carmakers. Very high brand loyalty and limited turnover in the sales force meant that customers were dealing repeatedly with the same corporate representative, thereby reinforcing brand loyalty. Most vehicles were special-ordered rather than sold from preexisting inventory. Close coordination between sales and production was possible with the same company owning both functions. The door-to-door sales system is being replaced in Japan with Western-style dealerships displaying large inventories and offering opportunities for test-drives. The transition has been generational since the late 20th century, with older people clinging to the traditional approach and younger people, preferring to visit dealerships before buying.

The long-standing structure of local franchised dealerships has inhibited the selling of vehicles through the Internet. Carmakers and dealers are permitted to provide consumers with information, including price, about vehicles available at particular stores. In response to a consumer inquiry, a dealer may send an e-mail stating a price for a specific vehicle. However, the transaction may not be completed through the Internet. The customer must go to the dealer to effect the transfer of money, papers, and keys to the vehicle. In the United States, an estimated 70% of new car buyers consult the Internet. Possession of information from the Internet and, in some cases, responses from multiple dealers have helped customers negotiate lower prices.

CHAPTER 5

Outside Market Forces

The most important outside market force for carmakers is the prominent role played by the manufacturers of the roughly 15,000 parts that go into the assembly of vehicles. Also of importance are suppliers of commodities and raw materials. Relations between carmakers and their suppliers have changed considerably in recent years because suppliers have more responsibility in the design and manufacture of vehicles than they had in the past.

Suppliers of Parts

A company making parts primarily destined for installation in new vehicles is called an original equipment manufacturer (OEM). A company making parts sold primarily as replacements in older vehicles is known as an aftermarket supplier. OEMs are responsible for more than 70% of the value added of a motor vehicle, totaling more than $1 trillion in annual sales worldwide.[1]

Original equipment can be classified into parts, components, systems, and modules. Terminology is not standardized, but the four types of equipment are commonly distinguished this way:

- A part is a small, individual piece, either a standardized generic item such as a bolt or a piece of metal, rubber, or plastic that is stamped, cut, or molded into a distinctive shape.
- A component consists of several parts put together into a recognized feature such as a seat cover or piston.
- A system combines several components to make a functional element of a vehicle such as an instrument panel or a transaxle.
- A module integrates several systems into one of a handful of major units of a vehicle such as a passenger compartment or engine.

OEMs are organized into a hierarchy called tiers. OEMs that sell directly to carmakers are called tier one suppliers. Tier two suppliers sell primarily to tier one suppliers, and tier threes to tier two suppliers. Carmakers have drastically decreased the number of their tier one suppliers from several thousands to a couple of hundreds. Traditionally, carmakers assembled vehicles from thousands of individual parts supplied by thousands of individual companies. For example, knobs, wires, tamped metals, and gauges were sent by different suppliers to the final assembly plants for fashioning into instrument panels. Now, a single supplier provides an instrument panel ready for installation in the vehicle. Suppliers of knobs and gauges have become tier two suppliers. A tier one supplier typically provides a system or module, and in turn obtains parts and components from tier one suppliers.

Types of Parts

Parts, components, systems, and modules can be allocated to five principal types or vehicle functions: powertrain, chassis, exterior, interior, and electronics.

Powertrain is the term that the motor vehicle industry employs to encompass the systems responsible for propelling the vehicle. The two principal powertrain systems are the engine and drivetrain. The heart of the engine is a block with several cylinders, most commonly four or six. Inside each cylinder is a piston that moves back and forth in four cycles or strokes as intake and exhaust valves open and close. The heart of the drivetrain is the transmission, which contains gears that are connected to the engine by means of an input shaft and to the axles by means of an output shaft. The purpose of the transmission is to adjust the input shaft to turn faster or slower than the output shaft, depending on conditions. Also part of the powertrain is the thermal system, which cools the engine and heats and cools the passenger compartment, and the exhaust system, including pipes and mufflers, to expel the spent gases.

The chassis makes a vehicle safe to drive and provides passengers with a comfortable ride. Principal chassis systems include fuel handling, driveline, steering, wheels, tires, brakes, and suspension. The fuel handling system includes a fuel tank, a fuel line to carry the fuel from the tank to the engine, a pump to push the fuel from the tank, and injectors to insert the fuel into the cylinders. The principal driveline components are the drive shaft and the axles. The drive shaft connects the transmission output shaft with the axles. The axles hold the wheels in place and drive them forward or backward. The steering system is the principal interface between the driver and chassis. The steering linkage makes the inside wheel turn more than the outside wheel. The wheels, which are mounted on the axles, are connected to the powertrain by the driveline and to the operator of the vehicle by the steering. A tire is attached to each wheel to make the movement of the vehicle smoother. Brakes, which are attached to the wheels, are controlled by a computer that is activated when the driver steps on the brake pedal. The suspension system, which includes springs, bars, and shock absorbers, stabilizes the vehicle, keeps tires on the road, and cushions passengers from uncomfortable bumps.

The exterior is the container that houses the other vehicle components and passengers. Principal exterior systems include the frame, body, bumpers, glass, and paint. The frame is constructed of steel members welded or riveted together, usually in the shape of a rectangle with crosspieces, sometimes in an X-shape. The body panels are stamped or pressed at stamping facilities from sheets of steel, aluminum, or plastic. Trim, such as door handles, grills, and mirrors, are attached to the body panels. The bumper typically includes a reinforcement bar sheathed in a plastic cover. Foam is packed between the bar and cover to cushion an impact.

The interior is the compartment that carries the passengers. Principal interior systems are the seats and interior trim. A seat includes a metal frame; foam padding; an external skin cut from fabric, leather, or vinyl and sewn to shape; and controls to adjust the seat. Interior trim consists of four principal modules: instrument panel, headliner, flooring, and doors. The instrument panel, housed in a soft-plastic dashboard, displays gauges that monitor and control the vehicle. Once made of woven fabric, the headliner and flooring are generally made of polyester fibers or composites that also include foam, cotton, and synthetics. Doors are sandwiches with an outer side stamped from metal and an inner side molded from plastic. Between the inner and outer panels are acoustical and restraint systems, locks, regulators, speakers, adjusters, wiring, and other electronic components.

The electronics control the performance of the vehicle and provide convenience to passengers. Electronics systems include engine management, entertainment, information, and safety. The growing role of electronics in motor vehicles is discussed in Chapter 7.

A count of several thousand individual manufacturing facilities operated by tier one suppliers in Europe and in North America was undertaken by a team including the author. The distribution by type of plant is similar in the two regions. Powertrain parts are produced at 34% of plants in Europe and 26% in North America. Exterior parts are produced at 18% of plants in North America and 10% in Europe. Chassis parts are produced at 19% of the plants and electronics parts at 16% of the plants in both regions and interior parts at 22% of the plants in Europe and 21% in North America. Thus, Europe has more powertrain plants and North America more exterior plants, whereas the share of plants making the other three types of parts is virtually the same in the two regions (Table 5.1).[2]

The share of suppliers in each of the five functions varies, depending on what is counted. Suppliers of exterior parts employ a relatively large number of people, whereas suppliers of powertrain parts have relatively high numbers of plants and value of shipments. In addition, some parts, classified as generic (such as bearings, brackets, and hinges), are found in more than one module and are not specific to motor vehicles.

Leading Parts-Making Companies

As a result of consolidation, the supplier industry is dominated by a relatively small number of very large OEMs. Seventeen suppliers had at least $10 billion in OEM parts sales worldwide in 2012, and five had at least $30 billion.

Table 5.1 Percentage of parts by type of system in Europe and North America

Plant location	Powertrain	Chassis	Exterior	Interior	Electronics
North America	26	19	18	21	16
Europe	34	19	10	22	16

Source: Compiled by author and Thomas Klier, Senior Economist, Federal Reserve Bank of Chicago.

The 10 largest suppliers together accounted for around $250 billion in OEM sales in 2012, that is, 20% of the global market, and the 100 largest had around $700 billion in OEM sales, that is 70% of the global market.

Despite consolidation, regional differences persist. Only two of the ten largest global suppliers ranked among the ten largest suppliers in each of the three major car producing regions of Asia, Europe, and North America. Four of the ten largest global suppliers were among the ten largest in two of the three regions, and four were among the ten largest in only one of the three regions.

The 10 largest OEM suppliers worldwide in 2012. Here are the 10 largest suppliers worldwide in 2012, grouped according to the regions of the world where they ranked among the 10 largest.[3]

- Among the 10 largest in Asia, Europe, and North America:
  - Robert Bosch GmbH, founded in Germany in 1886, produces a wide range of engine components, as well as brakes, steering, and exhaust systems. The company is owned by a charitable foundation and the Bosch family.
  - Continental AG was founded in Hanover, Germany, in 1871, to produce tires for carriages and bicycles. It is the world's fourth largest tire maker, behind Bridgestone, Goodyear, and Michelin, but it is a larger supplier than its tire rivals because it is also a major supplier of other parts such as brakes, suspension, and instrument panels.
- Among the 10 largest in Asia and North America but not in Europe:
  - Denso Corp., Japan's largest supplier, originated as Toyota's in-house electrical and radiator maker. It became an independent company in 1949, but Toyota still owns one-fourth of Denso and accounts for one-half of its sales.
- Among the 10 largest in Europe and North America but not in Asia:
  - Magna International Inc., based in Canada, is North America's largest supplier. The predecessor company was founded in 1957 by Frank Stronach, an Austrian émigré, to produce body stampings.

- ○ Faurecia, Europe's leading seat maker, was founded in 1914 by Bertrand Faure to make seats for Paris trams. It became one of the world's largest suppliers in 1997 when it acquired parts making activities that had been spun off from PSA Peugeot Citroën.
- ○ Johnson Controls Inc. (JCI) was incorporated in 1885 to make and sell thermostats to regulate building heat. JCI did not become a major car parts supplier until 1985 when it bought seat maker Hoover Universal, Inc. Into the 21st century, JCI was one of two leading seat suppliers globally, along with Lear Corp., the world's eleventh largest parts maker (see below).
- Among the 10 largest only in Europe:
  - ○ ZF Friedrichshafen AG was founded in 1915 by Ferdinand von Zeppelin to produce gears for Zeppelin airships. As a car parts supplier, the company has specialized in transmissions, axles, and other chassis systems and modules.
- Among the 10 largest only in Asia:
  - ○ Aisin Seiki Co., founded in 1949, is around one-fourth owned by Toyota. The supplier is closely tied into Toyota's *keiretsu* network, primarily as a supplier of engines and transmissions, and two-thirds of Aisin's sales are to Toyota.
  - ○ Hyundai Mobis originated in 1977 as a manufacturer of containers. It became a major car parts supplier in the 1990s, including the principal supplier of complete chassis modules to Hyundai and Kia. Mobis is part of the Hyundai *chaebol* through interlocking ownership.
  - ○ Yazaki Corp. was founded in 1929 by Sadami Yazaki to produce wiring for cars. The company, which is still family owned, is the inventor and leading supplier of wiring harnesses, which bundle together the large amount of otherwise chaotic wires that thread through vehicles.

Among the 10 largest suppliers in 2012 in one or two regions but not worldwide. These ten OEMs ranked among the ten largest in one or two of the three principal car-making regions but overall did not rank among the 10 largest globally.

- Among the 10 largest in Europe and North America but not in Asia:
  - Delphi Automotive Systems was GM's parts-making division until spun off as an independent company in 2000. As an independent company, Delphi has exited from most sectors in order to focus attention on electronics.
  - TRW Automotive is the leading supplier of steering gears. The parts maker had been part of a major military and aviation supplier until spun off as a separate automotive supplier in 2003.
- Among the 10 largest only in North America:
  - Lear Corp. was founded by William Lear as an aviation company. For the auto industry, it produced seat frames and became a major parts supplier in the 1990s through acquisition of several seat companies.
  - Cummins Inc. was founded in 1919 in Columbus, Indiana, to produce diesel engines. Carmakers manufacture most of their own engines, but a notable exception is diesel engines for pickup trucks in North America.
- Among the 10 largest only in Europe:
  - BASF SE was founded by Friedrich Engelhorn in Germany in 1865 to supply dyes. It now is a major supplier of styrenes and polyurethanes for molding plastic parts, as well as coatings.
  - Valeo SA was founded in France in 1923 to make brake linings. It has become Europe's leading producer of thermal systems, including heating and cooling.
- Among the 10 largest only in Asia:
  - Sumitomo Electric Industries was founded in Japan in 1897 to make copper wire. It started to supply wiring to the auto industry in 1961.
  - Toyota Boshoku Corp. was founded in 1918 in Japan to produce fabric and added car parts in 1972. The company

has become the integrator of complete interior modules for Toyota, including seats.

- ○ JTEKT Corp. was founded in Japan in 2007 through the merger of two Toyota *kereitsu* firms. It specializes in supplying Toyota with steering and driveline components.
- ○ Hitachi Automotive Systems was founded in Japan in 1930 to produce electric parts. It now specializes in engine controls and management systems.

Suppliers of Commodities

The auto industry is a leading purchaser of a variety of commodities and minerals. Purchases are made by both parts makers and carmakers. The average vehicle produced in the United States in 2011 weighed approximately 1,800 kilograms. Vehicles have been getting heavier by 6% between 1995 and 2000 and by 4% between 2000 and 2011. So carmakers have to purchase ever more commodities.

Steel is by far the most important component at 1,100 kilograms or 60% of the total weight (Table 5.2). Plastics and aluminum are next in importance, each about 9% of a vehicle's weight. Rubber and fluids account for 6% each of the weight of a vehicle and glass for 2%. Steel has been declining as a percentage of a vehicle's weight, from 68% in 1995 to 66% in 2000 and 60% in 2011. Plastics, aluminum, and rubber

Table 5.2 Percentage of raw materials by type in motor vehicles, 1995, 2000, and 2011

Type	1995	2000	2011
Steel and iron	68.1	66.3	60.1
Plastics	6.5	7.3	9.3
Aluminum	6.3	6.9	8.7
Rubber	4	4.3	5.5
Fluids	5.2	5.3	5.5
Glass	2.6	2.6	2.4
Other	7.3	7.3	8.5
Total weight (kg)	1,676	1,770	1,847

Source: Oak Ridge National Laboratory, *Transportation Energy Data Book.*

have increased their shares substantially, measured by percentage and by weight.[4]

Steel

The principal input in nearly all motor vehicles is steel. The amount of steel in an average vehicle increased through the 20th century, reaching an average of around 1,100 kilograms in 2000. Approximately one-fourth of steel produced in the United States is destined for motor vehicles.[5] Steel is rolled into a thin product through either hot rolling or cold rolling. Motor vehicle producers rely primarily on hot rolled steel for chassis components such as brake drums, wheels, and suspensions; body components such as cross and side members, roof frames, pillars, and doors; and drivetrain components such as transmissions, differentials, gearboxes, and clutches. Cold rolled steel is commonly used to stamp the hood, roof, fender, and door panels, because of its appealing surface finish.

Steel was not used in large quantities until the 1920s, when open wooden carriages were replaced with enclosed bodies. In the early 1900s, bodies were made primarily of wood. White ash was the most preferred. Philadelphia furniture maker Hale & Kilburn, then the dominant producer of steel seats for trains, is credited with producing the first steel car body for the 1912 Hupmobile. Hale & Kilburn's general manager Edward Budd set up his own firm in 1912 to produce steel car bodies and patented the all-steel car body. Budd's first large order came in 1914 from Dodge Brothers, which was then in the process of converting from the largest U.S. parts supplier to a high-volume carmaker.[6] Ford's decision to purchase Budd steel bodies in 1917 was a critical step in speeding up Model T production. The principal constraint in increasing assembly speed had been the time needed to paint the body. Paint applied to a steel body at a high temperature dried in a few hours, whereas varnish on a wood body took two weeks to dry. Budd was also credited with developing unitized body construction during the 1930s, three decades before it was widely adopted. During the Great Depression, Budd cut back on its body building business and developed stainless steel passenger railroad cars instead. Budd was acquired in 1978 by German steel manufacturer

Thyssen AG, which merged in 1999 with Krupp AG and sold its U.S. stamping operations in 2006 to a Canadian company Martinrea.

In the 21st century, the amount of steel in an average vehicle has been declining by around 5% during the first decade of the 21st century. The decline has been much more rapid for regular carbon steel, composed simply of iron and carbon, which accounts for 90% of steel production. The use of cast iron has also declined sharply. Nearly all engine blocks were once cast in iron, but increasingly, other materials are used to make the engine.

On the other hand, the amount of high- and medium-strength steel in an average vehicle increased by 50% during the first decade of the 21st century. High-strength steel—which is alloyed with other elements such as manganese, molybdenum, manganese, chromium, and nickel—is increasingly used by carmakers for body parts because it is stronger than regular steel. Because it is especially resistant to corrosion, stainless steel is used for a few components, such as the exhaust, for which resistance to corrosion is especially important.

Carmakers obtain around one-half of their steel from the integrated steel mills operated in the United States by four steelmakers: Arcelor Mittal, AK Steel, U.S. Steel, and Severstal. Arcelor Mittal, the world's leading steel producer by a wide margin, became the leading supplier of steel to the U.S. auto industry through acquisitions of Inland Steel in 1998 and International Steel Group in 2004. Of the world's six largest steel companies, only Arcelor Mittal owns mills in the United States. The other five—Nippon, Posco, JFE, Tata, and Shanghai Baosteel—are all based in Asia and have concentrated on the rapidly growing markets in Asia.

AK Steel sells a higher percentage of its output to the auto industry than do the other three leading firms. AK is the leading supplier of steel to the leading Japanese carmakers Toyota and Honda, although its largest customers are actually GM and Ford. Severstal is the fourth largest supplier of steel to the U.S. auto industry, holding 8% of the market.[7] Severstal owns the steel mill that was once integrated into the Ford Motor Company's massive River Rouge complex. In 2004, Severstal acquired the bankrupt Rouge Industries Inc., which Ford had set up as an independent company in 1989. Severstal's only connection today to Ford is the proximity of its mill. U.S. Steel is less heavily invested than its competitors in the auto industry.

The one-half of the car industry's steel purchases not made from the four integrated steel mills is divided about equally between imports and smaller steelmakers and minimills. Imported steel is shunned because of the high transportation costs of transoceanic shipping. Shortages in domestic production and currency exchange rate fluctuations can increase short-term reliance on imported sources. The principal channel by which foreign steel enters the U.S. motor vehicle industry is through service centers. Service centers purchase bulk quantities of steel from both domestic and foreign sources and perform finishing operations, such as cutting, shearing and grinding, that otherwise would have to be done by parts makers.

Carmakers are not major direct purchasers of steel from minimills in part because the steel products used in vehicles are stamped primarily from flat steel, which has not traditionally been a specialty of minimills. Steel produced from scrap at minimills has been regarded by the auto industry as insufficiently strong to stand up to the rigors of driving or at least to tests. Although it is not a major direct purchaser of steel from minimills, the auto industry gets some steel produced at minimills indirectly through service centers. The primary use of steel from minimills in the auto industry is for wiring.

Some automotive steel comes from intermediate processors, such as Shiloh Industries. Founded as a tool and die company in 1950, Shiloh sells $600 million worth of steel products to the auto industry. Shiloh manufactures blanks, which are two-dimensional shapes cut from flat-rolled steel. Shiloh cleans, coats, trims, and cuts steel into shapes that carmakers use to stamp into body panels such as doors and fenders. Blanks are also sent to other suppliers to stamp such parts as seat frames, bumpers, frames, and rails.

Although the motor vehicle and steel industries have been closely associated for a century, the relationship between them has often been uneasy. Carmakers once routinely sought bids for steel contracts from three companies; GM once negotiated with nine steelmakers. A savvy steelmaker would submit designs that, if adopted, placed it at a strategic advantage when manufacturing contracts were issued. The consolidation of the steel industry into a handful of larger firms has reduced competition. As the number of steelmakers willing to play the game declined, carmakers could no longer count on finding three bidders for contracts.[8] Just four steel companies at the table is too small for carmakers' comfort. The surviving steel companies have been independent and powerful enough to stand up to carmakers. For their part, carmakers have reduced steel content in favor of lighter-weight materials, notably plastic and aluminum, in order to increase fuel efficiency.

The fundamental divergence of interests between the two industries has been the price of steel. Essentially, low steel prices are good for carmakers and parts suppliers and bad for steelmakers, whereas high steel prices have the opposite effect. Policies such as tariffs and quotas on foreign imports designed to protect U.S.-based steel producers may limit the supply of steel and drive up prices, thereby harming U.S.-based car makers and parts suppliers. Conversely, open market policies may lower the cost of steel for the U.S. motor vehicle industry, but they expose the U.S. steel industry to foreign competition.

Other Commodities

Plastics and aluminum rank a distant second and third to iron and steel in automotive content, but the share of both is increasing rapidly. Rubber and glass round out the five most important commodities represented in motor vehicles.

The average plastic content of vehicles increased by one-third in the first decade of the 21st century, from 130 kilograms or 7% of vehicle weight in 2000 to 170 kilograms or 9% of vehicle weight in 2011. Plastics firms, such as BASF and Dow, supply the motor vehicle industry with commodities used to mold plastic parts. These include styrenes, polyurethanes, polypropylene, nylon, polymers, thermoplastic urethanes, and vinyls.

Plastics are durable, cheap to make, and lightweight. Plastic parts predominate in the interior systems, such as door panels, instrument panels, seat covers, headliners, and floor coverings. Smaller components are also plastic, including gauges, switches, vents, handles, floor mats, and seat belts. Plastic has replaced steel not only in exterior components, principally bumpers but also in some cases hood, trunk, and door panels. Some powertrain parts are also now plastic, such as the oil dipstick.

The amount of aluminum has increased from 41 kilograms in 1977 to 105 kilograms in 1995, 122 kilograms in 2000, and 161 kilograms in 2011, and the percentage has increased during that period from less than 1% to 9%. Aluminum is relatively expensive to cast, about $5.50 per kilogram compared with $0.90 per kilogram for iron in the early 21st century, so its increased use is adding several hundred dollars to the price of a vehicle. And it is not as durable as iron. Nonetheless, aluminum is being used more to cast engine blocks because it is an effective way to cut vehicle weight and thereby increase fuel efficiency.

In addition to engine blocks, the most common applications of aluminum are wheels and body panels, again because they reduce vehicle weight. Wheels were once made of steel, but aluminum wheels have captured the largest share of the wheel market because they are considered more stylish as well as lighter. The body panel most likely to be aluminum is the hood. The major supplier of primary aluminum and fabricated aluminum products to carmakers and suppliers is Alcoa, Inc.

Rubber is used primarily in tires. Also made from rubber are smaller parts such as wiper blades, engine mounts, seals, hoses, and belts. Around 75% of the world's natural rubber production is used to make tires for vehicles. Charles Goodyear mixed raw rubber with sulfur to create an elastic substance resistant to heat and cold, a process later called vulcanization. Until then, rubber's usefulness had been severely limited by its tendency to melt in summer heat and become brittle in winter cold. With the growth of motor vehicles in the 20th century, tires became the principal use for natural rubber. Synthetic rubber now accounts for 60% of the rubber content in tires.

Two-thirds of the world's original equipment tires are supplied by four companies: Bridgestone/Firestone Inc., Continental AG, Goodyear Tire & Rubber Co., and Michelin Tire & Rubber Co. Goodyear is the sole survivor of a number of tire companies that clustered in Akron, Ohio, in the early 20th century. Bridgestone, based in Japan, became the world's largest tire supplier when it acquired U.S.-based Firestone in 1988. U.S. Rubber and B.F. Goodrich merged in 1986 to form Uniroyal Goodrich, which was sold in 1990 to the French tire maker Michelin. General Tire was sold to German tire maker Continental in 1987.

Glass is used primarily on the front, side, and rear windows. The first glass windshield, introduced as an option in 1904, consisted of two horizontal panes of glass connected by hinges. The top half could be tipped open for an unobstructed view when the bottom half was completely splattered. The surface area of glass increased rapidly during the 1920s when the enclosed compartment replaced the open carriage. The introduction of laminated safety glass helped consumers overcome fear of the glass shattering. Glass is increasingly used in interior parts, such as navigation screens and back-up camera lenses.

The three leading glass suppliers worldwide are Asahi Glass Company, Saint-Gobain Group, and NSG/Pilkington. The three together have two-thirds of the world's automotive glass market. NSG/Pilkington and Asahi were two of four leading glass suppliers in North America. The other two were Glass Products (until 2007, Ford Motor Company's glass works) and Platinum (until 2007, PPG).

Distribution of Parts Suppliers

Most parts are produced in the same regional clusters as the final assembly plants. The clustering occurs at both the international and intraregional scales.

At the international scale, the largest suppliers are divided about equally among the three principal car-producing regions. The seventeen suppliers with at least $10 billion in OEM sales in 2012 included six with headquarters in Asia (five in Japan and one in Korea), six with headquarters in Europe (four in Germany and two in France), and five with headquarters in North American (four in the United States and one in Canada). The one hundred largest suppliers worldwide included thirty-five with headquarters in Asia (twenty-nine in Japan, five in Korea, and one in China), thirty-four with headquarters in Europe (twenty-one in Germany, three each in France and Spain, two in Sweden, and one each in Belgium, Italy, the Netherlands, Switzerland, and the United Kingdom), and thirty with headquarters in North America (twenty-six in the United States, three in Canada, and one in Mexico). In addition, one of the one hundred largest had headquarters in Brazil.[9]

The distribution of the leading suppliers changed sharply during the first decade of the 21st century. In 2000, seven suppliers had OEM sales over $10 billion, and these included five U.S.-based companies and one each in Germany and Japan. Thus, the growth of very large suppliers during the early 21st century has been entirely among companies based outside the United States. Similarly, the distribution of the hundred largest suppliers changed. The number with headquarters in Asia increased from twenty to thirty-five, including from nineteen to twenty-nine in Japan, from one to five in Korea, and from none to one in China. The number of large suppliers with headquarters in North America declined from forty-four to thirty, with the entire decline in U.S.-based firms. The number in Europe declined by only two during the early 21st century, but the distribution within Europe changed. The number of headquarters increased from seventeen to twenty-one in Germany, from none to three in Spain, and from none to one each in Belgium and the Netherlands. On the other hand, the number decreased from nine to three in France, from four to one in the United Kingdom, from three to two in Sweden, and from two to one in Italy. The loss of U.S. and European companies from the ranks of top suppliers is attributable primarily to their acquisition by surviving competitors as well as to relatively rapid expansion by suppliers in Germany and Asia.

Within the car-producing regions, parts suppliers are highly clustered. In North America, one-fourth of supplier plants are located within 250 kilometers of Detroit (the historic center of the region's auto industry), one-half are within 550 kilometers of Detroit, and three-fourths are within 1,000 kilometers of Detroit (Figure 5.1). The distribution of suppliers within Europe follows a similar pattern. One-fourth of supplier plants in Europe are located within 350 kilometers of Stuttgart, Germany (the center of that region's auto production), one-half within 535 kilometers of Stuttgart, and three-fourths are within 1,000 kilometers of Stuttgart (Figure 5.2). The figure of 1,000 kilometers is roughly equivalent to a one-day driving distance for truck deliveries.[10]

The degree of clustering varies by the type of part being produced. The historic core area of North American auto production in Michigan and adjacent jurisdictions is home to around 60% of body parts plants, 50% of powertrain and interior parts plants, and around 40% of chassis parts plants (Table 5.3). However, the core area has only 25% of electronics plants. Nearly one-half of electronics plants are in Mexico, North America's lowest wage area. Because of Mexico's lower wage rates, it is worthwhile for suppliers to incur the higher costs of shipping raw materials to Mexico and shipping assembled electronics parts back to auto alley where most of the customers (the assembly plants) are clustered.

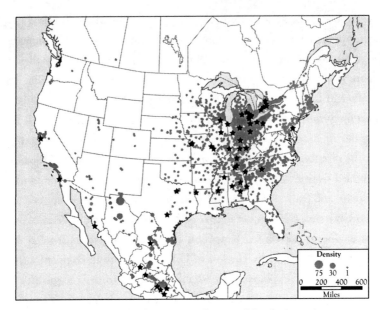

Figure 5.1 Distribution of parts suppliers in North America

Source: Compiled by author of Thomas Klier, Senior Economist, Federal Reserve Bank of Chicago.

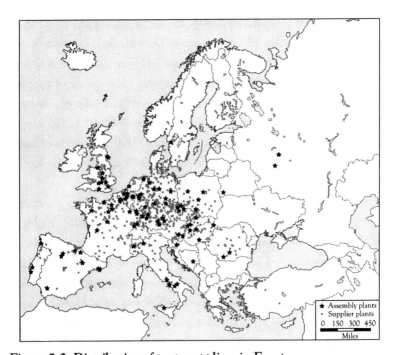

Figure 5.2 Distribution of parts suppliers in Europe

Source: Compiled by author of Thomas Klier, Senior Economist, Federal Reserve Bank of Chicago.

Table 5.3 Distribution of parts suppliers by type of part in North America

Region	Body	Chassis	Electronic	Interior	Powertrain	Total
Historic core	59%	39%	25%	49%	50%	669
First expansion	15%	24%	12%	16%	15%	249
Second expansion	12%	15%	44%	20%	14%	298
Peripheral	14%	22%	18%	16%	21%	275
Total	268	286	245	311	381	1491

Source: Compiled by author and Thomas Klier, Senior Economist, Federal Reserve Bank of Chicago.

Table 5.4 Distribution of parts suppliers by type of part in Europe

Region	Body	Chassis	Electronic	Interior	Powertrain	Total
Historic core	51%	55%	45%	48%	56%	998
First expansion	27%	21%	15%	22%	21%	405
Second expansion	14%	16%	19%	18%	13%	305
Peripheral	8%	7%	20%	12%	10%	213
Total	187	370	300	414	656	1927

Source: Compiled by author and Thomas Klier, Senior Economist, Federal Reserve Bank of Chicago.

Europe has much less variation by type of part. The core area centered on Germany and France contains around one-half of all parts plants, with little variation by type (Table 5.4). Around 20% of electronics plants are located in peripheral areas of Europe, compared to 11% for all plants, a much less extreme variation than in North America. In other words, whereas the low-wage area of Mexico has attracted a large percentage of North America's automotive electronics plants, the high-wage skilled labor area of Europe centered on Western Germany has retained a disproportionately large share of the region's electronics plants.

Changing Producer-Supplier Relations

Purchasing most parts from independent suppliers represents a reversal of the practice that prevailed through most of the 20th century. Ford and GM emerged in the 1910s as the two dominant carmakers in the United States and in the world in large measure because they made most of their parts in-house, an approach known as vertical integration. Historically, the motor vehicle industry was one of the world's most vertically integrated industrial sectors. Ford and GM were known for controlling all elements of the production process from raw materials through finished vehicles. Similarly in Europe, leading carmakers such as Fiat and Peugeot practiced vertical integration. As recently as the 1980s, GM produced more than 70% of its own parts and Ford 54%.[11]

After nearly a century of making most of their parts, U.S. and European carmakers turned most of their parts-making operations into independent businesses. Ford and GM exited within a year of each other, in 1999 and 2000, respectively. Vertical integration had become a liability rather than an asset because by then other carmakers were able to buy better quality parts from independent suppliers at lower prices. Though the level of vertical integration has declined sharply, yet it is still relatively high compared to most industrial sectors.

Manufacturers of key parts existed prior to the start of commercial production of motor vehicles in the 1890s. Carmakers relied on already established specialists for engines, transmissions, chassis, and bodies as well as for generic parts like nuts and bolts to put the other pieces together. Southeastern Michigan became the center of motor vehicle production in large measure because the leading manufacturers of key parts were already established there. Southeastern Michigan was especially important for early carmakers because it was the center of production for the most important part—the gasoline engine. Henry Ford and GM founder William Durant were both strong advocates of vertical integration. The two employed different strategies to achieve a high degree of vertical integration.

Ford sought direct control over all steps in the manufacturing process, from the mines and forests where raw materials were extracted to the rail lines that carried parts and vehicles to the dealers. Distrustful of others' competence and reliability, and unwilling to delegate responsibility, Ford set up from scratch most parts-making functions and clustered their operations in a single place. At Ford's complex along the River Rouge in the Detroit suburb of Dearborn, Ford famously unloaded at one end ships filled with iron ore from mines he owned, and at the other end loaded finished vehicles onto rail cars. In between, all but a handful of the parts were manufactured.

Prior to organizing GM in 1908, Durant had made Durant-Dort Carriage Co. the country's largest carriage maker largely through vertical integration. Durant believed that making parts was the key to getting production costs below those of competitors who purchased most of their parts. Consequently, Durant-Dort made its own bodies, wheels, axles, upholstery, springs, varnish, and whip sockets. As he transitioned from making carriages to making cars, Durant acquired for GM numerous parts suppliers as well as carmakers. Some proved liabilities, but others formed the foundation of GM's production and offerings. In some cases, entrepreneurs such as Albert Champion and Charles Stewart Mott were enticed to move to GM's hometown of Flint to set up parts facilities. In other cases, acquired companies were permitted to continue operations elsewhere in the country.

Under vertical integration practiced for most of the 20th century by Ford and GM, and to a lesser extent by Chrysler, companies making parts were relegated to secondary status in the production process. Each year, suppliers competed with each other for contracts from the Detroit three carmakers to produce parts according to precise specifications. The company submitting the lowest bid received a contract to supply a particular part for one year. To keep suppliers on their toes, GM in particular often bought the same part from several companies and deliberately changed suppliers of particular parts from year to year. Manufacturers did not share information with suppliers about how parts fit together or their intentions for retaining or changing individual parts in the future.

The impetus for changing carmaker–supplier relations during the late 20th century was the diffusion to North America and Europe of lean production from Japan. Before World War II, Japan's major parts suppliers were part of *zaibatsu*, which were large family-owned vertical monopolies, consisting of several industrial subsidiaries dominating specific sectors of a market, with a wholly owned banking subsidiary providing finance and a holding company providing top management.

During the U.S. occupation of Japan after World War II, the *zaibatsu* were replaced by *keiretsu*. The top management holding companies were eliminated, and the subsidiaries, including parts suppliers, became quasi-independent companies. However, under the *keiretsu* system, the quasi-independent companies are interrelated through cross-ownership. For example, Toyota holds equity stakes in engine supplier Denso, transmission supplier Aisin, seat supplier Toyoda Gosei, and interior trim supplier Koito, and the four parts suppliers hold equity stakes in each other.

Japanese carmakers adopted flexible production practices after World War II under the influence of W. Edwards Deming. One key element of flexible production is to give parts makers more responsibility in the production process. Key changes in carmaker–supplier relations have included:

1. Purchase of large systems and modules instead of individual parts: Systems, such as seats and suspension, are put together elsewhere and shipped as single deliveries by one supplier instead of hundreds of parts that would be put together at the final assembly plant.

2. Replacement of an annual contract with a multi year cooperative agreement covering the life of a particular model, typically 4 to 10 years: The supplier of one component could talk with the supplier of another component.

3. Selection of a supplier on the basis of its ability to meet quality standards instead of lowest cost: Suppliers submit to random audits and offer guarantees against defects and long-term warranties. Suppliers have to practice kaizen—continuous improvement in productivity, accident rates, inventory reduction, and other measures—to hit ever more ambitious quality and price targets. Instead of working to standardized blueprints, suppliers are given incentives to suggest improvements in carmakers' designs.

4. Transfer from the carmaker to the supplier of product development information that had once been considered confidential: Suppliers are involved in the planning process several years earlier than in the past. Electronic communications, such as computer assisted design,

foster flow of information between a supplier and a carmaker, as well as among various suppliers.

5. Expectation that the supplier establish research capabilities in order to take the lead in development of suitable components for future vehicles: Armed with the stability of long-term contracts, suppliers can invest more in design and engineering to improve the quality of parts and reduce production costs. For their part, carmakers have reduced their R&D capabilities in many aspects of components. Lower prices are achieved not by attacking suppliers' overhead margins but by working with suppliers to reduce production costs.

6. Delivery of needed components on a just-in-time basis instead of placing them in long-term inventory. Japanese carmakers use the term *kanban* to mean just-in-delivery. Logistics firms coordinate the movement of parts from suppliers to the final assembly plant in a logical sequence, often within only a few minutes of being needed on the assembly line.

7. Organization of parts suppliers into tiers with a relatively small number of so-called tier one suppliers selling directly to carmakers, tier two suppliers selling to tier one suppliers, and so on down a hierarchy of tiers. The number of tier one suppliers shipping directly to carmakers has been reduced by one-half since the late 20th century. Lower tier suppliers typically fabricate specific parts and lack engineering and research capabilities.

8. Consolidation of parts suppliers into fewer larger companies with capabilities of delivering entire integrated systems and modules instead of merely individual parts and components.

CHAPTER 6

Regulation of the Motor Vehicle Industry

This chapter focuses on government regulation of the motor vehicle industry. Government regulation of motorists and motor vehicles, as opposed to the motor vehicle industry, began in the first decade of the 20th century. Significant regulation of the motor vehicle industry dates from the 1960s. Governments have also played a more direct role in regulating the motor vehicle industry through ownership of carmakers.

Mandates

Safety and environmental concerns brought the imposition of mandates on carmakers. Since the 1960s, vehicles have been required to be equipped with devices that control noxious emissions, especially nitrogen oxide, particulates, and carbon monoxide. Since the 1970s, in response to periodic petroleum shortages and price rises, vehicles have been required to meet minimum fuel efficiency standards.

Safety Mandates

The United Nations World Forum for Harmonization of Vehicle Regulations has created uniform regulations on vehicle design. Although primarily aimed at promoting international trade in vehicles, the U.N. regulations promote uniform standards for several areas of vehicle safety, including lighting, crashworthiness, and instrumentation. The World Forum evolved from an agreement in 1958 by the Economic Commission for Europe, a U.N. agency that was established to promote trade across Europe by standardizing regulations. Non-European countries were allowed to join the forum in 1995. As of 2013, the agreement had been signed by 58 countries, including Japan, those in the European Union (EU), most of those once part of the Soviet Union, and most others in Europe. The most notable non signers are China, India, and the countries of North America, including the United States.

The watershed event in spurring U.S. government safety mandates was the publication in 1965 of *Unsafe at Any Speed*, written by Ralph Nader. Nader argued that carmakers, especially GM, were more concerned with making higher profits than with making their vehicles safer. The book interspersed lofty public statements by auto company executives about designing safe cars with descriptions of gruesome accidents that might have been prevented with the addition of inexpensive safety features.[1]

Nader cited examples from all three of the major U.S. carmakers, but his harshest criticism was directed at GM's Chevrolet Corvair. Nader charged that the Corvair had a tendency to roll over because of its design. The Corvair's engine was in the rear, so a relatively small percentage of the car's weight was in the front. As a result, the car tended to jackknife in sharp high-speed turns or crosswinds, inducing the driver to compensate by oversteering, resulting in loss of control. The first GM driver to test a Corvair prototype rolled it over. The first Ford driver to test a Corvair in 1960—companies routinely obtain early versions of competitors' models—also rolled it over, but Ford kept quiet about it for fear of retaliation by powerful GM against some of its own less-than-perfect vehicles. A stabilizing bar between the front wheels would have substantially reduced the risk of a rollover, but GM eliminated it in order to save $15 per vehicle. Equipping the Corvair with undersized tires saved another $1.

Stung by Nader's attack, GM officials fought back by trying to smear him. GM hired detectives to investigate Nader's background, credentials, and qualifications, not unusual in legal proceedings. When nothing damaging was found, a second more intensive investigation was ordered that exceeded the bounds of proper legal inquiry. Detectives tailed Nader and checked into his private affairs. They uncovered an ascetic—a man with a Harvard Law Degree living in near-pauper conditions in a rooming house in Washington—but instead GM spread stories that Nader was homosexual and anti-Semitic. Nader sued GM, settling out of court for $425,000, which he used to set up a consumer advocacy program that became a potent force in the consumer safety movement.

Placing profits ahead of safety was nothing new for GM. In 1929, GM president Sloan had been urged to introduce safety glass by officials from DuPont, which manufactured the plastic inner lining for the glass, but Sloan refused. He believed that the corporation had no responsibility for looking after the general welfare of the population. Corporations were ill advised to stray from their central mission of providing their shareholders with an acceptable rate of return on investment. The introduction of safety glass, Sloan argued, would significantly reduce the company's profits.[2]

In 1956, Ford decided to emphasize in its advertising the availability of a safety package called "Lifeguard Design." Seatbelts were a $16 option, $25 if bought in a package along with padded instrument panel and sun visors.[3] Ford along with Chrysler had made seatbelts an option in 1955, and sold 400,000 in the first 18 months of availability. With research showing that many accidents resulted in drivers being impaled on steering columns, Ford designed the steering wheel in a deep-dish shape to cushion drivers thrown forward in accidents. With research indicating that in one-fourth of accidents, motorists were thrown out of the car, Ford designed latches that kept doors closed during most accidents. Ford's safety campaign failed, as GM extended its sales lead over Ford in 1956 by featuring more powerful engines. Ford salvaged its 1956 sales by dropping the "Lifeguard Design" advertising campaign. The lesson for Ford and its competitors: safety doesn't sell. Motorists didn't want to be reminded that vehicles were dangerous or pay extra for safety features. Seatbelt usage would remain extremely low for another generation.

In the wake of the GM-Nader scandal, the U.S. Congress in 1966 enacted the National Traffic and Motor Vehicle Safety Act, which created the Department of Transportation and empowered the National Highway Safety Bureau (renamed the National Highway Traffic Safety Administration [NHTSA] in 1970) to set standards for automotive safety and order recalls of vehicles with safety-related defects. Vehicles were required to be built with safety features such as head rests, energy-absorbing steering wheels, shatter-resistant windshields, and safety belts. NHTSA also imposed safer standards on road design such as better lighting, guardrails, barriers separating oncoming traffic lanes, clearer delineation of curves through stripes and reflectors, and signs and utility poles that break away.

The 1972 Motor Vehicle Information and Cost Saving Act required NHTSA to set bumper standards. Bumpers had become standard equipment during the 1920s. They were originally thin metal strips designed to reduce damage to the vehicle from bumping into parked cars and pedestrians. By the 1950s, bumpers had become elaborate decorative features that caused as many injuries as they prevented. Beginning in 1972, NHTSA required bumpers to protect the fuel tank, headlamps, and other body and safety features during low-speed front-end impacts of 5 mph and rear-end impacts of 2.5 mph. The front-end standard was reduced to 2.5 mph in 1983.

Mandating safer roads and safer vehicles brought highway fatality rates down sharply in the United States. The number of fatalities declined from a peak of 55,000 in 1970 to 40,000 in 2000. The number of fatalities per 100 million miles driven in the United States, which had declined from 18 in 1920 to 5 in 1960 and 3 in 1980, declined further to 1 in 2000.[4] Rates of seatbelt usage increased from 11% in 1981 to 68% in 1997. In 1996, child restraints were used for 85% of children less than 1 year old and 60% of children aged 1–4 years.

Emissions Mandates

Carmakers are required to control the discharge of pollutants from the tailpipe. The three most significant emissions are hydrocarbons, nitrogen oxides, and carbon monoxide.

Photochemical smog is a haze that forms over urban areas, reducing resistance to respiratory infection and producing stinging in the eyes. It forms when hydrocarbons and nitrogen oxides from motor vehicles mix with sunlight. For each 1 kilogram of fuel burned in a vehicle, 0.2 kilograms of nitrogen oxides, and 0.1 kilograms of hydrocarbons would be discharged in the absence of emissions controls. Smog became more prevalent after World War II, in part because of the greatly increased concentration of vehicles in urban areas. Adding to the problem, cars built after World War II generated much more nitrogen oxides than prewar models because they had more powerful higher compression engines that ran hotter. The hotter oxygen and nitrogen in the cylinder air reacted to form nitrogen oxides, which were emitted through the exhaust pipe into the air. Exposure to carbon monoxide reduces the oxygen level in the blood, impairs vision and alertness, threatens those with pre-existing breathing problems, and can be fatal. In the absence of controls, 1 kilogram of burned fuel would generate 0.5 kilograms of carbon monoxide.

In the United States, the leading governmental entity in setting increasingly rigorous emissions standards has been the California Air Resources Board (CARB), which was established in 1967 through the merger of two other entities, the California Motor Vehicle State Bureau of Air Sanitation and the California Motor Vehicle Pollution Control Board. In 1961, the Bureau of Air Sanitation mandated that all vehicles sold in California from 1963 had to be equipped with technology known as positive crankcase ventilation that removed gases from the crankcase. In 1966, the Motor Vehicle Pollution Control Board adopted tailpipe emissions standards for hydrocarbon and carbon monoxide.

At the national level, the Federal Air Quality Act of 1967 established a framework for defining air quality control regions based on meteorological and topographical factors of air pollution. Most importantly, the act gave the State of California a waiver to set and enforce its own emissions standards for new vehicles based on California's claim that it had a unique need for more stringent controls. Other states may not enact their own emissions standards, but they do have the option of following California's more stringent standards rather than Federal standards. Thirteen states have chosen to follow the California standards: Arizona, Connecticut, Maine, Maryland, Massachusetts, New Jersey, New Mexico, New York, Oregon, Pennsylvania, Rhode Island, Vermont, and Washington.

The most important federal initiative to control pollution from vehicle emissions was the 1970 Clean Air Act, which called for the U.S. Environmental Protection Agency (EPA) to issue national air quality standards and specify required emission reductions. The EPA in 1971 called for 90% cuts in emissions of carbon monoxide and hydrocarbons by 1975 and nitrogen oxides by 1976. Compliance with the mandates was later pushed back to 1981. Rather than design entirely new engines, the carmakers met the standards through installation of catalytic converters. More recent initiatives have focused on reducing emissions through improving fuel efficiency, as discussed below.

California was also in the forefront of attempting to reduce global warming by regulating the emissions of greenhouse gases, especially carbon dioxide. In 2004, CARB adopted emissions standards for vehicles. Each carmaker needed to meet a standard based on a production-weighted fleet average, that is, the emissions of each of its vehicles weighted by its share of the company's total sales in a year. Increasingly stringent annual standards were set, measured in grams per mile. During the Administration of George W. Bush, the federal government opposed CARB's initiatives, but favorable court rulings and support from the Obama Administration removed the legal challenges to California to move ahead. The Federal EPA began regulating greenhouse gas emissions from vehicles in 2011 following California's pattern of increasingly stringent fleet-weighted averages. Fifteen other states opted to follow California's standards for controlling greenhouse gas emissions.

California and nine other states require zero-emission vehicles to account for 15.4% of the state's new car sales by the 2025 model year. In the absence of a nationwide standard, carmakers are coping primarily by selling only electric vehicles in the states with the mandate. "Compliance car" is the carmakers' informal name for these vehicles that they need to produce in limited quantities and sell at a loss such as Chevy Spark EV.[5]

The EU sets emissions policies, regulations, standards, and increasingly ambitious targets for Europe. In 2009, the EU set a target of 130 g/km (5.6 l/100 km or 42 mpg) for the average emissions of all new vehicles to be phased in by 2015. Each carmaker gets an individual annual target based on the average mass of all its new vehicles registered in the EU in a given year. Each carmaker had to ensure that 65% of its new vehicles registered in the EU in 2012 had average emissions below its target. The percentage of vehicles below the target would rise to 75% in 2013, 80% in 2014, and 100% in 2015. The EU has also set a target of 95 g/km (4.1 l/100 km or 57.6 mpg) for the overall vehicle fleet to be phased in by 2020.

EU member states decide how to best implement the standards. The EU encourageds member countries to establish variable tax rates for registering vehicles, with more fuel efficient vehicles benefiting from lower taxes.

Europe's standards for emissions have been adopted by China's State Environmental Protection Administration and India's Central Pollution Control Board under the Ministry of Environment & Forests. Japan has regulated emissions in urban areas, including nitrogen oxides since 1992 and particulates in 2001. Japan applies the standards to older vehicles, not just newly sold ones, requiring owners of older vehicles to either retrofit emissions controls or (more likely) replace them with newer models. Russia does not have an emissions mandate.

Fuel Efficiency Mandates

Minimum fuel efficiency standards are mandated by the governments of many countries. The initial impetus for these mandates in the United States was the oil price shocks of the 1970s. More recently, concerns for oil security have driven other developed countries to set higher fuel economy standards than those in the United States.

The United States produced more petroleum than it consumed during the first half of the 20th century. Beginning in the 1950s, the handful of large companies then in control of international petroleum distribution determined that extracting domestic petroleum was more expensive than importing it, primarily from the Middle East. U.S. petroleum imports increased from 14% of total consumption in 1954 to 58% in 2009. In 1960, several countries possessing substantial petroleum reserves created the Organization of Petroleum Exporting Countries (OPEC) in order to gain more control over the production and pricing of their resource. Countries possessing the reserves nationalized or more tightly controlled the fields, and prices were set by governments rather than by petroleum companies.

Angry at North American and European countries for supporting Israel during that country's 1973 war with Egypt, Jordan, and Syria, most OPEC members imposed an oil embargo in October 1973. Soon, gasoline supplies dwindled in the United States and much of Europe. OPEC lifted the boycott in March 1974 but raised petroleum prices from $3 per barrel to more than $35 by 1981. The rapid escalation in petroleum prices during the 1970s caused severe economic problems in North America and Europe. Production of motor vehicles, as well as steel and other energy-dependent industries, plummeted in the wake of the 1973–1974 boycott and price rise. Manufacturers were forced out of business by soaring energy costs, and the survivors were forced to restructure their operations to regain international competitiveness. In the wake of the 1970s shocks, the United States reduced its dependency on OPEC oil from 40% in the 1970s to 10% in the 21st century.

The principal U.S. policy response was the passing of the 1975 Energy Policy and Conservation Act, which mandated Corporate Average Fuel Economy (CAFE) regulations, effective in 1978. The sales-weighted harmonic mean fuel economy of a manufacturer's fleet of vehicles in a model year had to exceed a specified level, expressed in miles per U.S. gallon (mpg). Separate means were set for each carmaker's fleet of passenger cars and for light trucks. The EPA measures each vehicle's fuel efficiency, and the NHTSA enforces the standards. If the carmaker's overall CAFE fell below the standard, it had to pay a penalty. As a result of CAFE regulations, the average vehicle driven in the United States increased from 14 mpg in 1975 to 22 mpg in 1985. A National Academy of Sciences committee in 2002 concluded that CAFE regulations had improved vehicle efficiency by 14%.

In 2011, CAFE was changed from an average for each carmaker to a standard for each vehicle. A larger vehicle has a lower CAFE requirement than a vehicle with a smaller footprint. The overall average for all vehicles sold in the United States is anticipated to increase to 54.5 mpg in 2025.

The EU does not set a fuel economy mandate independent of the emissions mandate. The targets of 130 g/km in 2015 and 95 g/km in 2020 for the average emissions of new vehicles are considered equivalent to fuel efficiency of 42 mpg and 57.6 mpg, respectively.

Vehicles in China are assigned to sixteen weight classes, ranging from vehicles weighing less than 750 kg to those weighing more than 2,500 kg. Each vehicle must meet the standard of its weight class, or it cannot be sold in that model year. China does not permit corporate averaging. China's fuel efficiency standards are designed to secure an overall mean of 42.2 mpg in 2015.

Similarly, Japan allocates vehicles to fifteen weight classes. Fuel economy standards vary from 10.6 km per liter to 24.6 km per liter (24.9–57.9 mpg). However, as in the United States and Europe, Japan permits averaging fuel economy across all vehicles sold by a carmaker. The proposed overall average target for 2020 is 20.3 km per liter (47.8 mpg).[6]

Government Ownership

National and local governments own significant stakes of four of the ten largest carmakers through a variety of financial mechanisms. The two leading carmakers with direct government ownership are Renault and VW. Honda and Toyota have substantial indirect investment from the Japanese government. In no case, though, does a governmental entity exercise control over day-to-day management or strategic policy at the leading carmakers. Government ownership involvement in other carmakers, notably those in China, is more direct.

Renault was nationalized by the French government in 1945 at the end of World War II, in part because of Louis Renault's alleged collaboration with the Nazi during their occupation of France 1940–1944. During the nationalization period, Renault's finances were part of the national budget, and the national government absorbed the company's operating losses. Even under direct national government ownership, though, Renault was managed by executives who had latitude to run the company without direct government oversight. The government reduced its stake in Renault to 53% in 1994 and 46% in 1996, when it became a minority shareholder. The government now holds 15% ownership of Renault.

VW began as an initiative by the Third Reich to create a "people's car." After World War II, the company was reorganized as a trust controlled by the government of the Federal Republic of Germany and the government of the State of Lower Saxony. Though the national government no longer holds a direct stake in VW, Lower Saxony still owns 20%. In addition, the government of Qatar owns 17% of VW. The investment from Qatar came originally through an investment in Porsche, which is now owned by VW.

The Japanese government holds a substantial indirect financial interest in the leading Japan-headquartered carmakers. The connection is through the Japan Trustee Services Bank, which is the largest shareholder of Honda and Toyota. The Japan Trustee Services Bank in turn is owned two-thirds by Sumitomo Mitsui Trust Holdings and one-third by Resona Bank. Sumitomo Mitsui Trust in turn is owned one-third by the Resolution and Collection Corporation, which is a wholly owned subsidiary of Deposit Insurance Corporation of Japan, a semi-governmental organization. The

Resona Bank was rescued from insolvency in 2003 by the Japanese government, which as a result held two-thirds of the voting rights.

Three of the ten largest carmakers—Fiat, Suzuki, and GM—had substantial government ownership in the past. The government of Libya acquired 15% of Fiat in 1977. International outrage over Libya's support for international terrorism induced the Agnelli family to reacquire the shares from Libya. However, Libya has since repurchased 2% of Fiat shares. The government of India owned 18% of Maruti Suzuki when it was established in 1981. The Japanese carmaker Suzuki Motors has acquired an increasing share of the company, and the government sold all of its shares to financial institutions in 2007.

Government ownership of GM dates from the company's trip through bankruptcy in 2009. Sharp declines in sales and production during the severe recession of 2008–2009 left Chrysler and GM finances perilous. Unable to secure credit and running out of cash, the two carmakers turned to the U.S. government for assistance in late 2008. Rebuffed by Congress, the carmakers received emergency short-term loans authorized by President George W. Bush in his last month in office. Shortly after taking office in 2009, President Barack Obama appointed a Task Force to devise a strategy for dealing with the two carmakers near collapse. The two companies were restructured using a little-known and rarely used section of the U.S. bankruptcy code. Majority ownership of Chrysler was turned over to the United Auto Workers' Voluntary Employee Beneficiary Association (VEBA) health care retirement trust. Fiat was given operating control of Chrysler and permitted to buy more shares of the company by meeting several benchmarks. The restructured GM was initially owned 61% by the U.S. Government, 8% by the Government of Canada, and 4% by the Government of Ontario. Through public offerings of shares, the U.S. Treasury eliminated its holdings in several increments between 2010 and 2013.

Three of the ten largest carmakers not discussed in this section—Ford, Hyundai, and PSA Peugeot Citroën—remain under the control of the founding families. In the case of Hyundai, leaders of the *chaebol* have been active in South Korea's politics.

Several smaller and up-and-coming carmakers have substantial government ownership. Kuwait owns 8% of Daimler Benz. The leading Chinese carmakers are owned by the government of China.

CHAPTER 7

Challenges and Opportunities for the Motor Vehicle Industry

This chapter identifies future challenges faced by the motor vehicle industry in the production and sale of its product. On the production side, the principal challenge facing the motor vehicle industry is planning for the depletion of essential resources, especially petroleum. Most critical is the development and manufacture of alternatives to the gasoline-powered internal combustion engine. On the sales side, the principal challenge is adjustment to a rapidly shifting distribution of demand around the world. Motor vehicle sales are growing rapidly in some countries, especially in Asia, while prospects for growth are limited in Europe and North America.

Resource Depletion

The most fundamental resource depletion issue is the uncertain future of petroleum. The proven reserve of petroleum remaining to be extracted from conventional fields is limited. However, substantial reserves appear to exist in unconventional sources such as the Alberta, Canada, oil sands. But exploiting unconventional sources is strongly opposed by environmentalists because of the potential for adverse impacts. For example, oil sands (termed tar sands by environmentalists) are exploited through strip mining, which despoils the landscape and pollutes water supplies. Technically feasible alternatives to petroleum are available, but all carry significant economic penalties at this point in time, though the future may brighten for some of them.

Vehicles powered by electricity accounted for 40% of sales in 1900, and those powered by steam 38%. Only 22% of vehicles had gasoline-powered internal combustion engines that year. Electric vehicles were popular in large cities, especially as taxi cabs. But electricity became much more expensive than gasoline, especially after vast quantities of cheap oil were found in 1901 at Spindletop, Texas. Outside big cities, electric cars were not powerful enough to navigate the poor roads, and charging stations were rare (though some did exist). Steam power reached a technological dead end. In 1905, all but a handful of vehicle sales had internal combustion engines, and through most the 20th century, no realistic alternatives to gasoline power were offered for sale to consumers.

A century later, carmakers are again producing serious alternatives to gasoline-powered vehicles. Carmakers recognize that petroleum is a nonrenewable resource. While new fields are constantly being discovered, especially in unconventional sources, the prospects of reduced supplies and much higher prices for petroleum have spurred carmakers to hedge their bets by investing in alternative power sources. Government mandates discussed in the previous chapter for lower emissions as well as improved fuel efficiency add to the urgency for carmakers to identify alternative sources of power.

Numerous alternatives can be manufactured and displayed in dealers' showrooms. However, it is unclear which—if any—of the alternatives will ultimately prove financially rewarding to develop and which—if any—will attract enough consumers to justify the enormous investment. It is also unclear which technologies will continue to improve and which will end up as dead-ends. And while no technology is currently a money-maker, it is unclear which alternatives can be priced to return a profit in the long run and, therefore, are worth subsidizing in the short run. Not even the largest carmakers have sufficient resources to invest in all alternatives. So each carmaker is placing bets among the various alternatives in allocating scarce development and marketing resources.

The U.S. Department of Energy (DOE) identifies six types of alternative fuel vehicles: flex-fuel, diesel, hybrid electric, all electric and plug-in hybrid, micro hybrid, and gaseous and fuel cell. Flex-fuel and diesel involve making more efficient use of the remaining petroleum reserves. The other four alternatives are variations of electric power:[1]

- **Flex-fuel.** Ethanol is fuel made by distilling crops such as sugarcane, corn, and soybeans. Sugarcane is distilled for fuel in Brazil, where most vehicles run on ethanol. In the United States, corn (maize) has been the principal crop for ethanol, but this has proved controversial because the amount of fossil fuels needed to grow and distill the corn is comparable to— and possibly greater than—the amount saved in vehicle fuels. Furthermore, growing corn for ethanol diverts corn from the food chain, thereby allegedly causing higher food prices in the United States and globally. Ethanol production consumes 40% of the U.S. corn crop. More promising is ethanol distilled from cellulosic biomass such as trees and grasses. Factories producing cellulosic ethanol are expected to open in Iowa and Kansas in 2014.

- **Diesel.** Diesel engines burn fuel more efficiently with greater compression at a higher temperature than conventional gas engines. Most new vehicles in Europe are diesel powered, where they are valued for zippy acceleration on crowded roads as well as for high fuel efficiency. Diesels have made limited inroads in the United States, where they were identified with ponderous heavy trucks, poorly performing versions in the 1980s, and discharge of pollutants. Biodiesel fuel mixes petroleum diesel with biodiesel (typically 5%), which is produced from vegetable oils or recycled restaurant grease.

- **Hybrid electric.** In a hybrid vehicle, a gasoline engine powers the vehicle at high speeds, but at low speeds, when the gas engine is at its least efficient, an electric motor takes over. Energy that would otherwise be wasted in coasting and braking is also captured as electricity and stored until needed. Sales of hybrids increased rapidly during the first decade of the 21st century, led by Toyota's success with the hybrid Prius.

- **All electric and plug-in hybrid**. A full electric vehicle has no gas engine. When the battery is discharged, the vehicle will not run until the battery is recharged by plugging it into an outlet. In a plug-in hybrid, the battery supplies the power at all speeds. It can be recharged in one of two ways. While the car is moving, the battery can be recharged by a gas generator. When it is parked, the car can be recharged by plugging into an electrical outlet. The principal limitation of a full electric vehicle has been the short range of the battery before it needs recharging. Motorists can make trips in a local area and recharge the battery at night. Out-of-town trips are difficult because recharging opportunities are scarce. In large cities, a number of downtown garages and shopping malls have recharging stations, but few exist in rural areas. Using a gas generator to recharge the battery extends the range of the plug-in hybrid to that of a conventional gas engine.

- **Micro-hybrid.** A micro-hybrid vehicle is powered by a conventional gasoline engine. The micro-hybrid systems manage engine operation at idle.
- **Fuel cell.** Hydrogen forced through a PEM (polymer electrolyte membrane or proton exchange membrane) combines with oxygen from the air, producing an electric charge. The electricity powers an electric motor. Fuel cells are now widely used in small vehicles such as forklifts. Fuel cell vehicles are on the streets in a handful of large East and West Coast cities, where hydrogen fueling stations have been constructed.

According to the DOE, 2.5 million alternative fuel vehicles were sold in the United States in 2011. The total included 1.6 million with flex-fuel, 540,000 diesel-powered, and 250,000 hybrid vehicles. The other electric types had much lower sales, including 56,000 gaseous and fuel cell, 15,000 micro-hybrids, and 5,000 plug-in and all-electric vehicles. The DOE forecast in 2012 that 7.3 million alternative fuel vehicles would be sold in the United States in 2025, approximately 40% of total vehicle sales. The forecast includes 4.2 million with flex-fuel, 1.3 million micro-hybrid, 825,000 hybrid electric, 600,000 diesel, 319,000 plug-in and all-electric, and 86,000 fuel cell (Table 7.1). Indicative of the extreme volatility and uncertainty in forecasting future demand, the DOE just

Table 7.1 U.S. Department of Energy forecast of alternative fuel vehicle sales (in million vehicles)

Fuel type	2011	2025 estimate	2040 estimate
Flex-fuel	1.61	4.20	1.35
Diesel	0.54	0.60	0.63
Hybrid electric	0.25	0.82	1.08
Plug-in hybrid and all-electric	0.01	0.32	0.56
Micro-hybrid	0.01	1.31	5.18
Fuel cells	0.06	0.09	0.10
Total	2.48	7.34	8.91

Source: U.S. Department of Energy, Energy Information Administration.

2 years earlier had forecast a 50% market share for alternative fuel vehicles in 2020. Most auto industry analysts consider even the lower DOE forecasts to be too optimistic, given current projections for petroleum supply and price. On the other hand, hybrid vehicles got off to a slower start than plug-in and all-electric vehicles.

Petroleum is not the only natural resource with reserves of concern to the auto industry. Platinum is needed to manufacture catalytic converters and fuel cells. All but 3% of the reserves of this extremely rare metal are in South Africa. Lithium, essential for electronic devices, including electric-powered vehicles, is currently imported, primarily from Bolivia, although Wyoming may become an important source for the United States. China possesses 97% of the world's supply of rare earth elements.

Changing Markets

Prospects are bright for continued growth in demand for new vehicles. Worldwide sales are forecast to increase from 80 million in 2012 to 100 million in 2017. Although the high cost of vehicle production remains a significant barrier to entry for new companies, the forecast of continued substantial increases in global demand entices unprofitable and marginally profitable carmakers to remain in business. The arithmetic is compelling: the projected annual increase in worldwide vehicle sales is equivalent to the current level of sales of one of the current leading carmakers. In short, industry analysts expect enough growth to potentially satisfy every carmaker.

The principal challenge for existing and potential carmakers is adapting to changes in the market even in the midst of overall growth. The substantial worldwide increase in vehicle sales is based primarily on expectations in China. On the other hand, sales in North America are not expected to increase beyond the level achieved prior to the severe 2008–2009 recession, and sales in Europe are not expected to rebound even to the pre recession level. Carmakers are especially struggling to attract young people in Europe and to some extent North America.

Distribution of Demand

Vehicle sales are increasing rapidly in developing countries, especially in Asia, while stagnating in developed countries. In 1990, the five largest markets were the United States, Japan, Germany, France, and Italy. In 2020, only the United States will remain among the top five. From a peak of 19 million in 2007, vehicle sales in Europe (excluding Russia) declined to 14 million in 2012, and forecasts expect at best a modest increase in vehicle sales, though below the region's historic peak. Vehicle sales have also plummeted in Japan, from a historic high of 8 million to an anticipated 4 million in 2020. Only the United States is expected to show a slight improvement in the years ahead from its historic pre recession high.[2]

Joining the United States among the top five markets will be China, India, Brazil, and Russia. Vehicle sales in China increased from 600,000 in 1990 to 5 million in 2000 and 18 million in 2010, and they are forecast to reach 30 million in 2020. India's vehicle market has increased from 400,000 in 1990 to 700,000 in 2000 and 3 million in 2010 and is forecast to hit 11 million in 2020. Brazil's growth is less dramatic, from 700,000 vehicles in 1990 to 1 million in 2000, 3 million in 2010, and an anticipated 7 million in 2020. Russia's vehicle market is expected to double from 2 million in 2010 to 4 million in 2020.

Given the fundamental economic attraction of assembling vehicles near where they are to be sold, the shifting distribution of demand in the years ahead will result in the need for more production capacity in Asia and less in Europe. In principle, this seems like a straightforward calculation on the part of leading carmakers to close assembly plants in Europe and build them in Asia. But this is easier said than done. Closure of plants in Europe is extremely difficult because of the legal rights of workers. Opening of plants in Asia is also challenging because partnerships are needed with local carmakers and government agencies.

At this time, the best-selling vehicles in Asia come from leading international carmakers. China's sales are led by VW and GM. GM's Buick brand and VW's mass-market products have been especially popular in China at a time when both are struggling in North America. On the other hand, Japanese carmakers have had additional challenges in China because of long-standing political and military tensions between China and Japan, extending back to Japan's militaristic policies during World War II and more recently over control of a chain of small uninhabited islands known as the Senkaku in Japan and the Diaoyu in China.

In Europe and North America, where demand has not increased in the 21st century, the sale of vehicles to younger people has been especially stagnant. The mean age of buyers of new vehicles in the United States increased from 48 in 2007 to 51 in 2011. The median age increased more sharply in Europe, from 43 in 2006 to 46 in 2007 and 52 in 2011. The share of buyers of new vehicles who were under age 45 declined in the United States from 45% in 2007 to 33% in 2011. The decline was from 29% to 22% for buyers aged 35–44 and from 15% to 10% for buyers aged 25–34. On the other side, the percentage of all buyers of new vehicles aged 55–64 increased from 18% to 23%, and the percentage aged 65–74 increased from 9% to 13%. The trends are similar in Europe.[3]

The rapid aging of buyers of new vehicles affects all companies and makes about equally. The average age of buyers of the four best-selling makes—Ford, Chevrolet, Toyota, and Honda—was between 51 and 52 in 2011. A generation ago, Japanese-owned makes such as Honda and Toyota had significantly younger customers on average than did U.S.-owned makes such as Chevrolet and Ford. The average age is higher even for the customers of the higher priced makes of U.S.-owned companies—60 for Ford's Lincoln, 59 for GM's Buick, and 57 for GM's Cadillac.

Unclear to carmakers is the reason for the rapidly increasing age of new vehicle buyers in North America and Europe. Three possible explanations are offered:

- Lower birth rates since the late 20th century, combined with the aging of the baby boom generation born in the 1940s and 1950, have produced a short-term imbalance in the age distribution of the population in Europe and North America. Fewer vehicles are being sold to younger people because there are fewer of them in the population. Once the baby boom generation passes on in the 2030s, so this argument goes, the average age of new vehicle buyers will decline again.

- Younger people are buying fewer vehicles because they cannot afford them. The severe recession of 2008–2009 hit younger people harder than older people. The lingering effects of the recession in Europe have continued to depress demand among younger people, who have a higher unemployment rates and lower incomes than older people. Because of the poor economy, young people are more likely to delay moving out of their parents' home, getting married, and having children. Delays in obtaining a driver's license and buying a new vehicle are consistent with the pattern. Economic recovery, so this argument goes, will restore demand for new vehicles among young people.

- Interest in ever owning a new vehicle has declined among young people. Shiny stylish new motor vehicles are no longer viewed as "must have" products for younger people. Nor are they attracted by revving powerful engines, drag racing down Main Street, and making out at the drive-in movie. Vehicles are responsible for resource depletion and global warming. Young people will buy vehicles only to the extent necessary for practical errands, but, so this argument goes, the century-old love affair with the car is over.

The first two possible explanations are related to short-term demographic and economic cycles. It is the third of the explanations that most worries carmakers.

Performance and Connectivity

The most effective way to entice younger people in wealthy countries may be through in-vehicle electronics. Electronics comprise nearly 40% of the content of motor vehicles and the share is growing. The average new vehicle in 2011 contained more than 40 electronic controllers, five miles of wiring, and more than 10 million lines of software code, and the number of processors in vehicles was expected to double in 5 years. Electronics play two principal roles in motor vehicles: performance and connectivity. Performance has been the principal function of electronics, but connectivity will be of increasing importance in the future, especially for younger drivers.

Two aspects of performance have been especially impacted by electronics:

- Refining the powertrain to reduce emissions and improve fuel consumption: Examples include sensors linking the engine and transmission, electrically activated turbocharging, and electronic steering.
- Refining chassis, body, and interior to improve vehicle safety: Examples include airbags, electronic stability control, adaptive cruise control, and active lighting systems.

Connectivity was until recent years the distinctive function of the vehicle radio. Motorists stayed in touch with the outside world only by tuning the radio to news or entertainment programs provided by their favorite local stations. Now, everywhere they are, people demand instantaneous and continuous Internet connectivity and voice communications through their smartphones, tablets, and other portable electronic devices. "Everywhere" includes inside vehicles. Carmakers are still installing radios, but motorists expect other forms of connectivity. Of most importance to motorists are voice activated wireless communications, integration of their portable digital media players with the vehicle's entertainment system, and monitors on the instrument panel for clear display and control of the various connected devices.

Designing these connectivity functions has been especially challenging for carmakers. Instead of creating unique proprietary systems as they have in the past, carmakers need to permit connectivity inside the vehicle that is seamless with the portable electronics motorists are using in their homes, offices, and classrooms. The leading manufacturers of portable electronics are a new group of suppliers with whom carmakers must develop constructive partnerships.

The rapid pace of change of smartphones, tablets, and portable music players adds a further challenge. Carmakers make major changes in their vehicles every 4 to 6 years, whereas new versions of consumer electronics appear every year or so. Furthermore, vehicles are used for many more years than personal electronics, so carmakers must build in flexibility that minimizes obsolescence and accommodates future trends in personal electronics—to the extent that anyone can make accurate forecasts about these trends.

Given the high standards of design, assembly, and servicing for all contemporary vehicles, the ease of use of the connectivity system has become an increasingly important differentiator of consumer perception of quality. Carmakers increasingly market their vehicles on the basis of their distinctive approaches to connectivity.

Meanwhile, NHTSA considers driver distraction as a result of in-car electronics to be a major issue. In 2011, one-fourth of all accidents involved the use of cell phones. More than one-half of U.S. motorists admit to having used a cell phone while driving, and more than one-third have sent text messages. Text messaging, which is considered especially dangerous, has been banned in 39 U.S. states, yet more than three-fourths of young adults say that they can safely text while driving. Ten states have banned use of all hand-held devices while driving.

Carmakers expect greater integration of the connectivity function of vehicle electronics with performance, especially safety. Features being introduced into vehicles include:

- Cameras to make blind spots visible when the vehicle is backing up;
- Warnings when the vehicle leaves a lane;
- Communications with other vehicles to improve collision avoidance;
- Navigation systems that adjust the engine to the terrain;
- Systems that find and reserve parking and place the vehicle in a tight space.

Prototypes of driverless vehicles are now in service. The principal obstacles to their use are legal and behavioral rather than technological. The states of California and Nevada have legalized the use of driverless vehicles on public roads, but other countries and localities do not permit them. Unsettled is liability in case of an accident or a failure of a driverless vehicle. Would the fault lie with the carmaker, the motorist, or the vehicle owner? But given the predilection of so many motorists to use their electronics while driving, driverless vehicles could take care of the distracted driving problem.

Notes

Chapter 2

1. The number is 30,000 according to ask.com, and 5,000–7,000 according to yahoo.com. A study by the Australia Department for Environment and Heritage (2002) says 15,000.
2. *See* Rubenstein (1992), pp. 56–60, for more on the Selden patent, including the complete advertisement. The advertisement, as well as other information concerning the early years of the Ford Motor Company comes primarily from thousands of pages of depositions and testimony stemming from two legal cases. The first suit was initiated by two minority stockholders, John and Horace Dodge, to require Ford to pay higher dividends. The Dodge brothers charged that by repeatedly cutting prices and expanding production, Ford had sacrificed profits and paid low dividends. In 1917, Ford was ordered by the court to distribute over $19 million in dividends. After the decision, Henry Ford agreed to buy the shares of all of the minority shareholders, including the Dodge brothers. The minority shareholders refused to complete the transaction until they learned of their liability under the income tax law that had been created only a few years earlier with the ratification of the Sixteenth Amendment to the U.S. Constitution. The Commissioner of Internal Revenue set a valuation, the transaction was completed, but the Internal Revenue Service filed suit, claiming that even more tax was actually due.
3. Rae (1965), p. 59; Rubenstein (1992), p. 25.

Chapter 3

1. Clark (2012).
2. The most comprehensive history of Henry Ford and the Ford Motor Company is a three-volume work by Nevins (1954); Nevins and Hill (1957); Nevins and Hill (1962).
3. The most comprehensive study of GM's early years is Pound (1934). Cray (1980) and Keller (1989) studied mid 20th GM. Sloan published his memoirs in 1964. Durant himself left only a few papers, housed in the Kettering University library.
4. Gelsanliter (1990) reviews the arrival of the first Japanese-owned car plants in the United States.

5. *See* Laux (1976) for the early history of the French car industry, including Peugeot, Citroën, and Renault.
6. *See* Magee (2007) for more on Toyota's history.
7. *See* Rieger (2013) for more on VW's history.
8. North America and China production data from *Automotive News* and Europe production data from European Automobile Manufacturers' Association.
9. *See* Rubenstein (1986), pp. 288–300; Klier and McMillan (2006) for more on auto alley.
10. *See* Klier and Rubenstein (2011a) for more on the distribution of motor vehicle plants within Europe.

Chapter 4

1. Wang, Liao, and Hein (2012).
2. Estimates by the author based on United States, European Union, and Japan vehicle import and export data.
3. Sloan (1964).
4. Sales data from *Automotive News.*
5. LaReau (2013).
6. Rubenstein (2001), p. 284.

Chapter 5

1. *See* Klier and Rubenstein (2008) for more on parts suppliers.
2. Klier and Rubenstein (2011a).
3. *Automotive News* publishes an annual ranking of the largest suppliers in North America and worldwide.
4. Davis, Diegel, and Boundy (2013), p. 4–17.
5. Klier and Rubenstein (2008), p. 121.
6. Klier and Rubenstein (2008), pp. 92–93.
7. Klier and Rubenstein (2008), p. 125.
8. Klier and Rubenstein (2008), p. 126.
9. *Automotive News* annual ranking of the largest suppliers.
10. Klier and Rubenstein (2011a).
11. Klier and Rubenstein (2008).

Chapter 6

1. Rubenstein (2001), pp. 207–214.
2. Rubenstein (2001), p. 213.

3. Rubenstein (2001), p. 304.
4. Rubenstein (2001), p. 305
5. Collas (2013), p. 8.
6. For individual country information, see the United Nations Global Fuel Economy Initiative at http://www.unep.org/transport/gfei/autotool/about.asp

Chapter 7

1. U.S. Energy Information Administration (2013).
2. Chrysler (2011).
3. Libby (2012).

Resources for Further Study

Australia Department for Environment and Heritage. (2002). *Environmental impact of end-of-life vehicles: An information paper. Adelaide, South Australia: Australia department for environment and heritage.* Retrieved September 28, 2013, from www.environment.gov.au/settlements/publications/waste/elv/impact-2002/chapter4.html

Boas, C. W. (1961). Locational patterns of American automobile assembly plants. *Economic Geography 37*(3), 218–230.

Chrysler, M. (2011). *Forecast calls for sharp rise in global demand through 2020.* Retrieved September 28, 2013, from WardsAuto: http://wardsauto.com/ar/forecast_global_demand_110216

Clark, J. (2012). *Mondo Agnelli: Fiat, Chrysler and the power of a dynasty.* Hoboken, NJ: John Wiley & Sons.

Collas, M. (2013, June 22). New EV will test the range of GM's plug-in strategy. *Automotive News,* p. 8.

Cooney et al. (2009). *U.S. motor vehicle industry: Federal financial assistance and restructuring. CRS Report for Congress* (Report number R40003). Washington, DC: Congressional Research Service.

Crabb, R. (1969). *Birth of a giant: The men and incidents that gave America the motorcar.* Philadelphia, New York, and London: Chilton Book Company.

Cray, E. (1980). *Chrome colossus: General Motors and its times.* New York, NY: McGraw-Hill Book Company.

Davis, S. C., Diegel, S. W., & Boundy, R. G. (2013). *Transportation energy data book.* Oak Ridge, TN: Oak Ridge National Laboratory.

Demings, W. E. (1994). *The new economics for industry, government, education.* Cambridge, MA: MIT Center for Advanced Educational Services.

Editors of Automobile Quarterly. (1971). *The American car since 1775.* New York, NY: Dutton.

Epstein, R. C. (1928). *The automobile industry: Its economic and commercial development.* Chicago, NY: A.W. Shaw Co.

Flink, J. J. (1988). *The automobile age.* Cambridge, MA, and London: The M.I.T. Press.

Gelsanliter, D. (1990). *Jump start: Japan comes to the heartland.* New York, NY: Farrar, Straus, Giroux.

Halberstam, D. (1986). *The reckoning.* New York, NY: William Morrow and Co.

Hurley, N. P. (1959). The automobile industry: A study in industrial location. *Land Economics 35*(1), 1–14.

Ingrassia, P., & White, J. B. (1994). *Comeback: The fall and rise of the American automobile industry*. New York, NY: Simon & Schuster.

Keller, M. (1989). *Rude awakening: The rise, fall, and struggle for recovery of general motors*. New York, NY: William Morrow.

Keller, M. (1993). *Collision: GM, Toyota, Volkswagen, and the race to own the 21st century*. New York, NY: Currency Doubleday.

Klier, T. (2009). From tail fins to hybrids: How Detroit lost its dominance. *Economic Perspectives 33*(2), 2–17.

Klier, T., & McMillen, D. (2006). The geographic evolution of the U.S. auto industry. *Economic Perspectives 30*(2), 2–13.

Klier, T., & McMillen, D. (2008). Evolving agglomeration of the U.S. auto supplier industry. *Journal of Regional Science 48*(1), 245–267.

Klier, T., & Rubenstein, J. (2008). *Who really made your car? Restructuring and geographic change in the auto industry*. Kalamazoo, MI: W.E. Upjohn Institute for Employment Research.

Klier, T., & Rubenstein, J. (2011a). Configuration of the North American and European auto industries—a comparison of trends. *European Review of Industrial Economics and Policy 3*.

Klier, T., & Rubenstein, J. (2011b). What role did regional policy play in addressing the US auto industry crisis? *International Journal of Automotive Technology and Management 11* (2), 189–204.

Klier, T., & Rubenstein, J. (2012). Detroit back from the brink? Auto industry crisis and restructuring, 2008–2011. *Economic Perspectives 36*(2), 35–54.

Klier, T., & Rubenstein, J. (2013). Restructuring of the U.S. auto industry in the 2008–2009 recession. *Economic Development Quarterly 27*(2), 144–159.

LaReau, J. (2013). *Record store profits—and more to come*. Retrieved September 28, 2013, from Automotive News: http://www.autonews.com/article/20130708/RETAIL07/307089961/record-store-profits----and-more-to-come#

Laux, J. M. (1976) *In first gear: The French automobile industry to 1914*. Kingston, ON: McGill-Queen's University Press.

Libby, T. (2012). *Buick goes against trend and attracts younger buyers*. Retrieved September 28, 2013, from http://blog.polk.com/blog/blog-posts-by-tom-libby/buick-goes-against-trend-and-attracts-younger-buyers

Magee, D. (2007) *How Toyota became #1: Leadership lessons from the world's greatest car company*. New York, NY: Penguin Books Ltd.

May, G. S. (1975). *A most unique machine: The Michigan origins of the American automobile industry*. Grand Rapids, MI: William B. Eerdmans.

Nader, R. (1965). *Unsafe at any speed*. New York, NY: Grossman.

Nevins, A. (1954). *Ford: The times, the man, the company*. New York, NY: Charles Scribner's Sons.

Nevins, A., & Hill, F. E. (1957). *Ford: Expansion and challenge 1915–1933*. New York, NY: Charles Scribner's Sons.

Nevins, A., & Hill, F. E. (1962). *Ford: Decline and rebirth 1933–1962*. New York, NY: Charles Scribner's Sons.

Pound, A. (1934). *The turning wheel*. Garden City, NY: Doubleday, Doran & Company.

Rae, J. B. (1965). *The American automobile: A brief history*. Chicago, NY: University of Chicago Press.

Rattner, S. (2010). *Overhaul—An insider's account of the Obama administration's emergency rescue of the auto industry*. New York, NY: Houghton Mifflin Harcourt.

Rieger, B. (2013). *The people's car: A global history of the Volkswagen Beetle*. Cambridge, MA: Harvard University Press.

Rubenstein, J. (1986). Changing distribution of the American automobile industry. *Geographical Review 76*(3), 288–300.

Rubenstein, J. (1992). *The changing U.S. auto industry*. London, UK: Routledge.

Rubenstein, J. (2001). *Making and selling cars: Innovation and change in the U.S. automotive industry*. Baltimore, MD: The Johns Hopkins University Press.

Sloan, A. P. (1964). *My years with General Motors*. Garden City, NY: Doubleday.

Taylor, F. W. (1914). *The principles of scientific management*. New York, NY: Harper.

U.S. Energy Information Administration. (2013). *Annual energy outlook 2013*. Washington, DC: U.S. Department of Energy.

Vlasic, B. (2011). *Once upon a car: The fall and resurrection of America's Big Three auto makers—GM, Ford, and Chrysler*. New York, NY: HarperCollins.

Wang, A., Liao, W., & Hein, A. P. (2012). *Bigger, better, broader: A perspective on China's auto market in 2020*. New York, NY: McKinsey & Company.

Weber, A. (1929). *Theory of the location of industries*. (translated by C. J. Fredrich). Chicago & London: The University of Chicago Press.

Wells, C. W. (2012). *Car country: An environmental history*. Seattle, DC: University of Washington Press.

Womack, J. P., Jones, D. T., & Roos, D. (1990) *The machine that changed the world*. New York, NY: Rawson.

Index

CPSIA information can be obtained at www.ICGtesting.com
Printed in the USA
BVOW02s1117200114

342331BV00005B/17/P